I put my trust in you.

PSALM 56:3

"In a culture that combats fear with believe-in-yourself strategies, Kristen equips believers with biblical truth to actively fight fear by loving Christ more. I'm grateful for such a practical tool to help me preach truth to myself."

—RUTH CHOU SIMONS, bestselling author of *GraceLaced* and *Beholding and Becoming: The Art of Everyday Worship*

"Kristen will show you how to fight fear: See more clearly who God is, hear more fully what He promises, and match what you see and hear to the things you fear the most. Forget the futility of trying to work up strength and courage you know you don't have, and find biblical hope in this honest, realistic, and perceptive book."

—COLIN S. SMITH, senior pastor, The Orchard; president, Unlocking the Bible, unlockingthebible.org

"I encounter women almost daily who are facing paralyzing fears of every kind. The agony is written on their faces. They know God is greater than their fears, but it's puzzling how to trust His promises in the midst of real-life, knock-me-down heartache. Kristen Wetherell's *Fight Your Fears* is a must-read book for anyone battling the enemy of fear. It's packed with theological truth minus the Bible-story pat answers. It leads us to the cross of Christ to overcome fear by cultivating the right kind of fear—fear of the Lord. Rather than making us feel guilty for having anxiety, it offers gospel hope as the key to freedom from its bondage. *Fight Your Fears* receives my highest recommendation!"

—LESLIE BENNETT, manager of Women's Ministry Initiatives, Revive Our Hearts

"Too often, Christians live with an incomplete definition of fear. We either think courage means a life of false bravado and 'living our truth,' or we succumb to an unhealthy fear of men and circumstances. Finally, there is a book that tells us what God's Word says about this important subject, a book that points us toward a confident faith in the Christ who has conquered all things. If worry has paralyzed your soul, this book will help you both fight unhealthy fears and embrace the fear of the Lord. Those of us who too often live scared lives can find freedom and walk tall in the power of God. And Kristen Wetherell helps us do that."

—DANIEL DARLING, vice president of communications, The Ethics and Religious Liberty Commission and author of several books, including *The Dignity Revolution*

"With biblical insight, relatable context, and powerful challenges, Kristen Wetherell accomplishes her goal: not to make her readers less afraid but more afraid of what's right to fear. It's difficult to walk away from this book without feeling conviction about our disordered fears and the comfort available to those who fear God."

—LORE FERGUSON WILBERT, author of *Handle with Care*

"Fear of God is perhaps one of the least understood—and most distorted—teachings in the Christian faith. Some are paralyzed by it, while others reject it altogether. In the midst of this confusion, Kristen Wetherell has written a clear and thoughtful guide. With the heart of a teacher, Kristen identifies the key to sorting out this difficult topic and points us to a better way."

—SHARON HODDE MILLER, author of *Free of Me: Why Life Is Better When It's Not about You*

"*Fight Your Fears* doesn't promise to take away your anxiety but instead offers something more valuable—to help you trust God when you're afraid. Steeped in Scripture, this book will help you fight your fears through remembering God's character, reciting his faithfulness, and resting in his promises. As you do, you'll be drawn to the Savior, confident that he'll never fail you."

—VANEETHA RENDALL RISNER, author of *The Scars That Have Shaped Me: How God Meets Us in Suffering*

"In theory, we should have fewer fears than any generation before us. We are surrounded by security systems, advanced medicine, organic food, and endless information on glowing rectangles in our pockets. And yet, it turns out, even 'sophisticated moderns' are scaredy-cats. What's wrong with us? Why are we so deeply, miserably afraid? Will we ever find relief from the worries that hum beneath the surface of our lives? Questions like these haunt us, which is why I am so grateful for Kristen Wetherell's timely new book. With piercing clarity and concrete counsel, she takes us by the hand and leads us over slippery terrain to the Rock of ages. I will be recommending *Fight Your Fears* widely to others, and returning to it often myself."

—MATT SMETHURST, managing editor, The Gospel Coalition; author of *Before You Open Your Bible: Nine Heart Postures for Approaching God's Word*

"Kristen has written a compassionate and helpful resource, pointing us to our source of help and courage. Calling us to lift our eyes from the ground to the sky, Kristen shows us a God that is infinitely more powerful than our deepest fears and whose care for us is tender, gentle, and kind."

—LAURA WIFLER, cofounder, Risen Motherhood; podcaster; coauthor of *Risen Motherhood: Gospel Hope for Everyday Moments*

fight
your
fears

fight your fears

TRUSTING GOD'S CHARACTER AND
PROMISES WHEN YOU ARE AFRAID

KRISTEN WETHERELL

BETHANY HOUSE

a division of Baker Publishing Group
Minneapolis, Minnesota

Published by Bethany House Publishers
11400 Hampshire Avenue South
Bloomington, Minnesota 55438
www.bethanyhouse.com

Bethany House Publishers is a division of
Baker Publishing Group, Grand Rapids, Michigan

Printed in China

Library of Congress Cataloging-in-Publication Control Number: 2019944958

ISBN 978-0-7642-3437-8

Cover design by Brand Navigation
Interior design by William Overbeeke

Author is represented by the Gates Group.

20   21   22   23   24   25   26   7   6   5   4   3   2   1

To my faithful parents,

Jennie and Ed:

The Lord Jesus has used you mightily
to teach me to fear him and cherish his Word.
I love you both!

CONTENTS

FOREWORD

L ONG AGO, a counseling professor taught me that fear lies at the core of any unhelpful or ungodly reaction. The scales fell from my eyes in that moment, and I saw how fear had lurked beneath many of the repetitive sinful patterns of my life, pulling the strings that led me to control, lash out in anger, and even turn inward under heavy self-condemnation. I'd done anything and everything I felt might protect my own heart from pain, but by not naming my responses as fear, I'd nurtured it, fueled it, and used it as a weapon in relationships.

Naming fear, I soon discovered, was only the first miniscule step. I had to claim and confess it as self-idolatrous sin, a soul-eating plague rather than the silly, inconsequential plaything I'd made it. Fear, in other words, had inflamed my pride and made God impotent and small. Fear had told me lies about God my entire life and, cleverly enough, kept me from the very One who could drive fear from my heart.

Because love drives out fear, and God is love.

You may wonder, as I did, what love has to do with it. I would much prefer an ability to control the future or to avoid the pricks and pains of life. I'd like a security I can see and touch and a sure plan on exactly how everything is going to turn out well in the end. But the Bible says perfect love is the way fear is cast out, and what this means is that *God's demonstration of love* is the way fears are conquered.

The more I have risked drawing close to God, believing he accepts me as fully as he accepts Christ, the more I've known security. I've learned to tell him my fears without wondering if he's impatient with me, and more importantly, *I've learned to tell my fears about God*. Like a child facing a bully on the playground, I eyeball them and say, "My dad is bigger and stronger than yours, and he is always for me."

Perhaps you are just now recognizing that fear strikes at the heart of what you do or how you respond to others, or maybe you've known fear all your life. Perhaps you fear God himself, and not in a good way. Perhaps you've been so hurt by other people that you've hardened a shell of protection around yourself. Perhaps you fear you won't have enough, whether it's love or capacity or food to eat. No matter where you are, I'm so glad you're going to read these words from Kristen. She does what is needed: She gives us God himself. She tells us about him so that we can tell our fears about him too. So read, savor, and soak in the truths of who he is, friends, and let his perfect love fight your fears to their death.

—Christine Hoover
Author of *With All Your Heart: Living Joyfully through Allegiance to King Jesus*
www.gracecoversme.com

INTRODUCTION

From One Fearful Person to Another

When I am afraid, I put my trust in you.

Psalm 56:3

WHAT IF I told you that your problem with fear isn't that you are too afraid but that you aren't afraid enough?

And what if I told you that your goal isn't to become fearless?

I'll bet that you and I could fill this page with a list of our fears. Fears about the future; fears about our health, jobs, and families; fears about inadequacy and failure (or maybe success); fears about how much *fear itself* seems to affect our decisions, plans, and growth in the Christian life.

And fears about what God thinks about our fears.

I'm not coming from a place of having totally figured this out and wanting to impart my secrets to you here, but as a fellow Christian who is fighting the good fight alongside you.

Fears color my thoughts on a daily basis: *Will my daughter and I be safe today as we're out and about? What if someone breaks into our house tonight? What if my Lyme disease comes back?* We all have lingering fears that we can't seem to shake. And then there are more acute fears connected to circumstances: *What if our plane is hijacked? What news will the doctor deliver today? What if my boss tells me I'm fired? What if . . .*

The what-ifs are never ending.

The enemy of our souls uses fear as a killjoy and peace-stealer, blinding us to what is ours in Jesus Christ, and I am convinced that the methods we often employ to deal with our fears are unrealistic and powerless to help us.

That's one of the reasons I wrote this book.

What This Book Won't Do

When it comes to fear, there are a few qualifications we should make. First, we cannot deal with fear simply by choosing fearlessness. Often, we look within ourselves for strength and bravery (or we look to self-help experts, who tell us to look within ourselves). But the trouble with this is that *we are the problem*. Looking within ourselves for a solution to fear is like a drowning swimmer trying to scrounge up more energy when what they need is rescue. Self-help is a powerless method of dealing with fear.

Second, our ultimate goal in fighting fear is not to become fearless, but to know and love and *fear* the One who empowers us in the fight. The Christian life certainly includes the benefits and blessings of walking with Jesus (such as the power to fight fear), but it's *knowing Jesus* that is our primary aim. When fearlessness is our aim, it's easy for us to see him as a means to this end, as some kind of divine self-help expert who can aid us in reaching our goals. Instead, in our fight against fear, our ultimate goal is to know and love and *fear* Jesus. We'll focus on this goal throughout the book.

Third, fighting our fears is a process that tends to happen gradually. Yes, Jesus has completely broken fear's power, but this does not mean that fear is no longer a problem for those who have faith in him. Has Jesus defeated sin and the devil? No doubt. And can Jesus do an astounding and dramatic work in our souls to free us from certain fears? Absolutely. But the issue remains that Christians live in a now-but-not-yet reality, and while sin's power is indeed broken, its presence is ongoing. Sanctification—transformation into Christlikeness—happens gradually. The expectation that *Jesus automatically equals fearlessness* is unrealistic and therefore can be defeating for Christians who can't seem to overcome their fears.

So here's what this book won't do: It most likely won't help you become fearless.

That's what some other books on fear will promise you—but that's not the way the Christian life generally works. God gives us all kinds of commands that are impossible for us, in our own strength, to keep:

- "Go, and from now on sin no more" (John 8:11).
- "Rejoice in the Lord always" (Philippians 4:4).
- "You therefore must be perfect, as your heavenly Father is perfect" (Matthew 5:48).

So when Jesus says, "Fear not" and "Do not be afraid," he knows full well that we won't obey him perfectly. We will continue to struggle with fear in this life. But that's exactly why we need him. That's why he came—to do the impossible for us. To give us what we need to obey his commands. To rescue us and give us grace and power to fight our fears.

To help us know him, trust him, treasure him, glorify him, *fear him.*

And that's my prayer for this book: not that it will promise total elimination of your fears, but that God will use it to help you fight your fears as you learn to trust his character and promises.

Fear and God's Word

The Christian life is a battle, and Scripture calls itself a sword. When we are afraid, what we need isn't powerless self-help, misdirected goals, or an overpromise; what we need is an effective weapon with which to fight our fears. We need *truth*. So many fears are rooted in untruths that we must wield God's powerful, unchanging Word of truth against what we're thinking and feeling. We must fight the good fight with "the sword of the Spirit, which is the word of God" (Ephesians 6:17). We must fight fear with an even greater fear.

So here's where we're going: First, we'll explore the problem of fear. *Where does fear come from? Is all fear bad? What is the key to becoming less fearful?* Then we'll open God's Word to see *who he is*, and after that, *what he's promised*, specifically six of God's precious and very great promises (2 Peter 1:4) that directly address six of our greatest fears.

We'll see how the antidote to fear isn't self-esteem or fearlessness but our great God and Savior, Jesus Christ, who is worthy to be feared.

Each chapter will seek to answer two questions: "How is this promise fulfilled in Jesus?" and "With the help of Christ, how can I learn to trust this promise?" At the end of each chapter, we'll get practical with how God's promises equip us to fight fear, adapting some concepts from Puritan preacher John Flavel's book *Triumphing over Sinful Fear*:

- **Ponder:** We'll memorize verses to wield in our fight against fear.
- **Preserve:** We'll consider who God is and how he's been faithful.
- **Prepare:** We'll think about how God promises to be with us in the future.
- **Pray:** We'll respond in praise, confession, and thanksgiving and ask God for his help.

Fear Not

Friend, all of God's promises apply to you when you are united to his Son by faith. Jesus Christ purchased his people by his blood shed on the cross, and when you trust in him, everything that's his becomes yours, including all the promises of God that he fulfilled. My senior pastor, Colin Smith, says, "Your strategy for fighting your fear will be to confront it by looking through it and beyond it to Jesus Christ and putting your trust in him."[1] If you've never considered him before now, I pray you will find in Jesus all you've been searching for and that this book will help you do that.

So consider your fears: Are you afraid of what tomorrow might bring? Of the diagnosis? Of putting food on the table and a roof over your family's head? Are you scared of what other people think of you? Does the reality of death terrify you?

Then you're in the right place. When God commands us to "fear not" in Scripture, thankfully that command comes with a promise: "What is impossible with man is possible with God" (Luke 18:27). Let's trust that promise and begin.

the problem of fear

one

one

I AM GOD

(When You Aren't Afraid Enough)

The friendship of the Lord is for those who fear him, and he makes known to them his covenant.

Psalm 25:14

MY FIRST GOAL in this book isn't to help you feel less afraid—it's actually to make you *more* afraid. Let me explain: The root of our problem with fear isn't that we are too afraid, but that we aren't afraid enough of the God who is worthy to be feared.

Recently, I had a conversation with a woman who seemed certain about her ideas of God. She explained that God lives in every one of our souls and that he's whatever each religion says he is. These seem like two different viewpoints, but they have the same foundation: *God is whomever we want him to be.*

This is a common belief. Our contemporary culture celebrates a definition of "god" that works for the individual, calling ultimate truth an imposition and an attack upon human freedom. We are all on our own spiritual journeys, people say, and therefore, we will all have our own grasp of who God is.

But what if the truth about God is absolute and clear? What if we don't need to wonder about him because he has revealed himself to us?

This would change everything, and it has. We can know who God is because he has told us in our Bibles. Far more than a history book or pages of information, the Bible is God *speaking*, revealing to us precisely who he is so we're not left guessing and groping around in the dark. Pastor and theologian Jonathan Edwards once said, "'Tis rational to suppose, that when God speaks to the world, there should be something in his word or speech vastly different from men's word."[1] And there is—our God communicates with us uniquely and powerfully through Scripture, which is this "vastly different" word. It is God's inspired Word that is without error: "All Scripture is breathed out by God and profitable for teaching, for reproof, for correction, and for training in righteousness, that the man of God may be complete, equipped for every good work" (2 Timothy 3:16–18).

We can know, without a doubt, who God is *because he has told us.*

The Beginning of Wisdom

When it comes to knowing what we're afraid of and why we're afraid, the truth that God speaks to us in the Bible matters. Since God has wonderfully revealed himself to us through his Word, our exploration of fear must start and end by looking at him, not at ourselves. Of course, this seems counterintuitive: *Don't I need to look at myself to grasp why I'm afraid?* But like any sick person who can't discern the nature of their sickness, and who can't heal apart from a doctor's diagnosis and treatment, we must look to the Great Physician for help and healing. We must begin with the God who speaks.

This is why it is such good news that God hasn't left us wondering about him but has revealed himself through his Word. We'll only see ourselves rightly if we see him rightly, and we'll only learn to fight our fears as we learn of God and listen to his diagnosis and treatment—his very words. This is why King Solomon wrote in Proverbs 9:10, "The fear of the Lord is the beginning of wisdom, and the knowledge of the Holy One is insight."

Do you want insight into your fears? Do you want wisdom about how to fight them? True wisdom and insight are found in learning to fear God.

God, Who Is Worthy to Be Feared

So then, let's take a look at some verses that tell us who God is. If you're like me, when you see a large chunk of Scripture in a book, you might be tempted to skim these or skip them altogether. But I encourage you not to. Read these verses slowly and carefully. Let them sink in.

> Who is like you, O Lord, among the gods? Who is like you, majestic in holiness, awesome in glorious deeds, doing wonders?
>
> Exodus 15:11

The adversaries of the Lord shall be broken to pieces; against them he will thunder in heaven.

1 Samuel 2:10

Will not his majesty terrify you, and the dread of him fall upon you?

Job 13:11

Your righteousness, O God, reaches the high heavens. You who have done great things, O God, who is like you?

Psalm 71:19

Your kingdom is an everlasting kingdom, and your dominion endures throughout all generations.

Psalm 145:13

Have you not known? Have you not heard? The Lord is the everlasting God, the Creator of the ends of the earth. He does not faint or grow weary; his understanding is unsearchable.

Isaiah 40:28

It is he who made the earth by his power, who established the world by his wisdom, and by his understanding stretched out the heavens.

Jeremiah 51:15

Oh, the depth of the riches and wisdom and knowledge of God! How unsearchable are his judgments and how inscrutable his ways!

Romans 11:33

He who is the blessed and only Sovereign, the King of kings and Lord of lords, who alone has immortality, who dwells in unapproachable light, whom no one has ever seen or can see. To him be honor and eternal dominion. Amen.

1 Timothy 6:15–16

"I am the Alpha and the Omega," says the Lord God, "who is and who was and who is to come, the Almighty."

Revelation 1:8

What do these Scriptures tell you about God? That his character is unblemished, his works are wonderful, his justice is perfect, and his purposes cannot be thwarted. That the Creator who delicately knit you together in your mother's womb also formed the depths of the sea and the heights of the mountains. That the Maker who fashioned the tiniest of insects also designed the entire solar system, and that the Almighty One who said, "Let there be" in the beginning upholds it all to this day. Our God is awesome in power, unmatched in wisdom, and beautiful in his glory. He is transcendent and holy, holy, holy—above and apart from all things.

God's holiness leads us to recognize our lowliness before him. John Calvin said that "man is never sufficiently touched and affected by the awareness of his lowly state until he has compared himself with God's majesty."[2] When we glimpse God in his greatness, we can't help but wonder along with King David, "What is man that you are mindful of him, and the son of man that you care for him?" (Psalm 8:4). God is not like us; he is holy and awesome. When we behold God's majesty and hear testimonies of his greatness in Scripture, there is only one right response, and it's the response he intends for us to have: The God of the universe is infinitely worthy to be feared.

What Is the Fear of God?

And what does this kind of fear look like? The fear of the Lord means *to worship God with the reverence and awe his glory deserves.*

Since the creation of man, God's intention was that we fear him. Out of the overflow of God's infinite fullness, he created us to walk closely with him in love and obedience (Genesis 1:26–27; 3:8) and to be in perfect fellowship with him and with one another. God wasn't obligated to make anything—he was fully satisfied in himself[3]—rather, he desired to share himself with, and reflect himself through, all he would make. So his incomparable perfections overflowed in a life-giving display of creativity and generosity. God made, and it was good (Genesis 1:31). The only fear humankind knew was of the One who made them—*a worshipful reverence and awe of his glory.*

In Deuteronomy 10, Moses beautifully describes this good and godly fear:

> And now, Israel, what does the Lord your God require of you, but to fear the Lord your God, to walk in all his ways, to love him, to serve the Lord your God with all your heart and with all your soul, and to keep the commandments and statutes of the Lord, which I am commanding you today for your good?
>
> vv. 12–13

To fear God means we desire him above all else. It means we follow him eagerly, out of love. It means we serve him, and him only, with all of our strength, trusting his character and purposes and obeying his words. It means we worship him with the reverence and awe his glory deserves.

Yet, when I look at this passage it's clear to me that I *don't* fear God as I ought, that no one does, for that matter.

If fearing him means walking in all his ways and loving him with all my heart and soul, then I've failed miserably.

We all have.

Distorted Fear

God's beautiful glory beckons us to respond in worshipful fear, but something has gone seriously wrong. Rather than revere him, our world defames him. Rather than delight in him, we worship ourselves and the things God has made. And rather than obey him without question, we do so only when it's convenient for us—

No, we do not fear God as we ought to. Instead, we fear anything and everything he has made.

What happened?

When Adam and Eve ate the forbidden fruit, sin entered the world and corrupted everything, including what and whom we fear.[4] Because of sin's effects, God gave us a protective response system for legitimate dangers, what John Flavel calls *natural fear*. Natural fear "is not always sinful," Flavel says, "but it is always the fruit and consequence of sin."[5] There's a reason that firefighters wear suits, zoo animals require cages, meteorologists warn against hurricanes, and our protective instincts kick in when our kids are in danger. These are fearful situations brought about by sin's brokenness, and God has given us the ability to respond accordingly. Jon Bloom describes this as God's mercy:

> When fear moves us to avoid things that are truly dangerous, we experience just how merciful a gift it can be. God created fear to help keep us free. He meant it to protect us from all manner of real harm so we can remain as free as possible to live in the joy he intended.[6]

Even as sin corrupted creation, our merciful God gave us instincts against its fruit, and we should be thankful for this gift of protective, natural fear. At the same time, we should mourn for what sin did to the human soul. Sin turned awe of God into terror before him, reverence into rebellion against him, and worship of God alone into idolatry. *Sin distorted the fear of the Lord.*

We see this in Adam and Eve's response to their disobedience as they hid from their Creator, with whom they previously had walked in fellowship. Instead of going to God for forgiveness, "the man and his wife hid themselves from the presence of the Lord God among the trees of the garden" (Genesis 3:8). If God had not sought out the couple, Colin Smith writes, they would have remained hidden:

> The natural sequel to sin is not repentance, but hiding. The sinner's first impulse is to run from God.[7]

Can you think of a time you tried to hide your sin from God or ran from him? I see this response in our young daughter, who runs away and pretends she doesn't hear us when she has done something wrong. The fear of the Lord that was intended for our joy and freedom—worship with reverence and awe—sin has twisted into something enslaving, something condemning. Sin makes us unholy enemies of a holy God as we attempt to hide ourselves from what our sin deserves.

Terrified Fear of God's Wrath

To be God's enemy is the most terrifying of all fears "for the wrath of God is revealed from heaven against all ungodliness and unrighteousness of men" (Romans 1:18). The consequence of Adam and Eve's sin was physical and spiritual death, alienation from their Creator, and the corruption of the creation—all of which we inherited, and all of which make us God's enemies and condemn us before him: "Therefore, just as sin came into the world through one man, and death through sin, and so death spread to all men because all sinned . . . one trespass led to condemnation for all men" (Romans 5:12, 18).

God's wrath is his right and just response to the sin that offends his holiness. In John Stott's words, "God's holiness exposes sin; his wrath opposes it. So sin cannot approach God, and God cannot tolerate sin."[8] The doctrine of sin is unpopular in our world and even our churches because it is offensive, difficult to swallow, and intimidating, as it should be. But to ignore or belittle the reality of God's wrath doesn't mean it disappears. To deny it is our *death*. R.C. Sproul writes,

> Do we consider the wrath of God as a primitive or obscene concept? Is the very notion of hell an insult to us? If so, it is clear

that the God we worship is not a holy God: Indeed He is not God at all.[9]

God is holy, and sin is anything but. God created us to commune with him, but instead we cower. Sin twisted the fear of our Creator from worshipful reverence and awe of him into rebellion against him, idolatry, and as a result, terror before him. The once awesome fear of the Lord has become awful to us—

And when we no longer fear God as we ought, the result is that we fear lesser things too much.

The root of our problem with fear isn't that we're too afraid, but that we aren't afraid enough of the One who is to be feared.

Learning to Fear God

If the fear of God means worshiping him with the reverence and awe his glory deserves, and if sin has distorted this fear, then where do we go from here? What hope is there for sinners who have chosen our own way and idolized lesser things, placing ourselves under the terrifying wrath of God and bearing the fruit of fears upon fears?

How can we learn to be afraid in the best way and return to a good and right fear of the Lord?

We can't—not on our own, at least. But nothing is impossible with God. He seeks the guilty and ashamed, inviting us out of hiding and into the fear-exposing light of his presence. He grants us a glimpse of his greatness, and a grasp of our lowliness, that leads us to fall on our knees and cry out for his mercy and forgiveness. The God who is to be feared is also the Great Physician, who is more than able to work a miracle in us, healing what has been distorted by sin.

Our all-powerful, infinite, awesome God gives us this wonderful promise in Psalm 25:

> For your name's sake, O Lord,
>> pardon my guilt, for it is great.
> Who is the man who fears the Lord?
>> Him will he instruct in the way that he should choose.
> His soul shall abide in well-being,
>> and his offspring shall inherit the land.
> The friendship of the Lord is for those who fear him,
>> and he makes known to them his covenant.
>
> vv. 11–14

Those who confess their sin to God—"pardon my guilt, for it is great"—know the beginnings of what it is to fear him. Those who come to him with a broken and contrite spirit, the Lord promises to instruct. And those who acknowledge their lowliness before him will be ready to receive the covenant of his friendship, secured by the precious blood of Jesus Christ.

To him, we turn next.

LEARNING TO TRUST

PONDER. Memorize Psalm 25:14: "The friendship of the Lord is for those who fear him, and he makes known to them his covenant."

PRESERVE. How have you related to God in the past? How do you relate to him right now? What words would you use to describe him?

PREPARE. To see ourselves rightly, we must see God rightly, and he uses his Word to show us who he is and who we are. How could you make Bible reading a more consistent part of your every day?

PRAY. *Holy God, there is no one like you. You and you alone are perfectly righteous, infinitely wise and powerful, and without limits. I know I have not feared you as your holiness deserves. Make me more and more aware of the sin within me that offends you. Give me a desire to seek you through your Word, to know you truly, and to fear you as you always intended me to. Show me my need for your intervention, that only you can change me, and lead me to Jesus. In his name, amen.*

The friendship *of the* Lord *is for those who* fear *him, and he makes known to them his* covenant.

PSALM 25:14

two

I HAVE SAVED YOU

(When You Fear Condemnation)

There is therefore now no condemnation for those who are in Christ Jesus.

Romans 8:1

Tʜᴇ ꜰᴇᴀʀ ᴏꜰ condemnation—the terror-based fear that comes as a result of rejecting God and remaining under his just wrath—lurks within each of us. We may not recognize it that way, but it's there. As we have seen, it's the reason we try to justify ourselves when we sin, or hide our sin from others. It's equally the reason we're paralyzed by our sin, weighed down, even depressed, by the guilt and shame of it. It's the (often unbeknownst) motivation behind our culture's rejection of the reality of sin. And in those who have trusted Jesus Christ for salvation, it's behind our struggle to grasp that God's promise of forgiveness and grace can be ours on the basis of Christ alone, not on anything we do.

This fear of condemnation is a deeply personal fear. I often feel that a looming gray cloud follows me around, heavy laden with my insufficiencies and sins. Usually without realizing it, I've believed lies about who God is, convinced that he must be generally disappointed in me. I fear that my Bible reading isn't robust enough, that my prayer time isn't sincere enough, and that my growth in holiness isn't what it should be. When my sins are before me, I feel like a failure.

Does this fear of condemnation resonate with you? I'd argue that we all experience it to some degree. We'll explore it now, as we carefully examine two accounts from Scripture, two mountain scenes that will help us address this fear and return to a right fear of the Lord.

The First Mountain

Imagine you're an Israelite, one of God's chosen people. You've witnessed the Lord's great power against the Egyptians when Moses parted the seas to rescue you from slavery (Exodus 14:31). Here in the wilderness, you've seen God turn bitter water into sweetness (Exodus 15:25) and provide food from heaven (Exodus 16:15). Now Moses tells you that God will descend upon Mount Sinai in three days, and you will meet him there. *You will meet the Almighty.*

What do you feel at the thought of this? What does it mean for a mere human to meet the Holy One? Scripture tells us what happened that day:

On the morning of the third day there were thunders and lightnings and a thick cloud on the mountain and a very loud trumpet blast, so that all the people in the camp trembled. Then Moses brought the people out of the camp to meet God, and they took their stand at the foot of the mountain. Now Mount Sinai was wrapped in smoke because the Lord had descended on it in fire. . . . And the whole mountain trembled greatly.

Exodus 19:16–18

This divine visitation at Mount Sinai was terrifying. Even when God mercifully wrapped himself in a thick cloud, his presence was overwhelming, causing the people to tremble and the very mountain along with them:

Now when all the people saw the thunder and the flashes of lightning and the sound of the trumpet and the mountain smoking, the people were afraid and trembled, and they stood far off and said to Moses, "You speak to us, and we will listen; but do not let God speak to us, lest we die." Moses said to the people, "Do not fear, for God has come to test you, that the fear of him may be before you, that you may not sin." The people stood far off, while Moses drew near to the thick darkness where God was.

Exodus 20:18–21

The sight of God's power and majesty—his entrance by fire and smoke, the disorienting blare of a trumpet, the mountain storm—was so awful that Israel pleaded, "Do not let God speak to us. We can't bear it." They asked Moses to be God's spokesman for fear of dropping dead at the sound of a word from the Almighty's lips.

Matthew Henry writes of their request, "Ever since Adam fled, upon hearing God's voice in the garden, sinful man could not bear either to speak to God or hear from him immediately."[1] This was Israel's experience that day. To them, God was a holy and refining fire that threatened to consume them, despite Moses drawing near to him on their behalf—and who can play with fire without being burned? Their response was to stand far off and tremble in fear.

A Second Mountain

Now imagine you're at another mountain. Rather than remaining at the foot of it, you are led up its paths by Jesus. You've been walking closely with him, seeing him perform miracles and teach about his kingdom. You've grown close to Jesus, learning of him, and you're convinced he is the Christ, the Son of the living God.

Here, on this mountain, you see Jesus as you've never seen him before. He looks like himself, yet is suddenly changed. In an instant, his clothes become radiant and dazzling, white as light, causing you to shield your eyes and hide your face. His brightness is blinding, more beautiful than anything you've ever seen. And he has unexpected visitors: Moses and Elijah appear, talking with him.

As if his transfigured presence before you isn't overwhelming enough, a bright cloud suddenly overshadows you and a voice comes out of the cloud: "This is my beloved Son, with whom I am well pleased; listen to him." God Almighty speaks, and his words utterly level you. You fall face-first to the ground in terror—

Until someone touches you. It's Jesus, who says, "Rise, and have no fear." You look up and see no one but him.[2]

Similar, Yet Different, Scenes

What do you observe about fear, as described in these two mountain scenes? Remember that the fear of God means worshiping him with the reverence and awe his glory deserves, and that sin has distorted this good fear, making us enemies of God and bringing us under his wrath. What we see in these accounts reflects the latter kind of fear: We observe sinful humans in terror before a sinless God, overwhelmed by the awful dread of the Holy One. John Stott comments on our inability to draw near to God by reflecting on the images of fire and light in these accounts: "Both discourage, indeed inhibit, too close an approach [to God]. Bright light is blinding; our eyes cannot endure its brilliance, and in the heat of the fire everything shrivels up and is destroyed."[3]

While these two mountain scenes share the above similarities, they also have a few major differences—and understanding them is paramount for our grasp of how we return to a right fear of God.

First, the position of the people. Moses tells the Israelites to prepare to meet with God—but they must remain at the foot of Mount Sinai and must not touch the mountain unless they have a death wish. Matthew's gospel, however, tells us that the disciples ascend the mountain with Jesus, unknowingly close to his transfiguration and an encounter with God. It's the presence of the person of Christ that makes the difference here.

Second, the presence of God. In Exodus, Mount Sinai is swallowed by darkness, fire, smoke, and a thick cloud as God descends upon it to speak with Moses and deliver the Ten Commandments. He protects Israel from hearing his voice directly, and still they plead to be spared from it. On the other mountain, however, we're told that God's cloud is "bright" (Matthew 17:5) and that he speaks audibly to the disciples.

Third, the person of the mediator. Two versions of "do not fear" are spoken in these accounts. Moses' words come with a warning: The people don't need to fear death by God's consuming fire that day, but they do need to fear him by obeying his commands every day. The Ten Commandments are given that their lives may reflect and honor God, and to show them their need for rescue when they continue to sin and fail. But Jesus' response is different: "Rise, and have no fear," he says.

Why so simple and straightforward?

Mediators of God's Covenant

A passage in the book of Hebrews will help us answer this question. Notice how its first few verses perfectly describe the Israelites at Mount Sinai:

> For you have not come to what may be touched, a blazing fire and darkness and gloom and a tempest and the sound of a trumpet and a voice whose words made the hearers beg that no further messages be spoken to them. For they could not endure the order that was given, "If even a beast touches the mountain, it shall be stoned." Indeed, so terrifying was the sight that Moses said, "I tremble with fear." But you have come to Mount Zion and to the city of the living God, the heavenly Jerusalem, and to innumerable angels in festal gathering, and to the assembly of the firstborn who are enrolled in heaven, and to God, the judge of all, and to the spirits of the righteous made perfect, and to Jesus, the mediator of a new

covenant, and to the sprinkled blood that speaks a better word than the blood of Abel.

Hebrews 12:18–24

Our two mountain scenes are represented here. In them, Moses and Jesus act as mediators between God and humans. A *mediator* is one who stands in the chasm that sin has caused to renew God's covenant relationship with his people and bring about reconciliation and peace. In the Old Testament, this covenant relationship meant that God made promises to Israel that depended upon them fearing him—worshiping him with the reverence and awe his glory deserves. But God's covenant was continually broken by their irreverent rebellion and sinful idolatry. Stott summarizes Israel's history well when he writes,

> God had entered into a covenant with Abraham, promising to bless him with a good land and abundant posterity. God renewed this covenant at Mount Sinai, after rescuing Israel (Abraham's descendants) from Egypt. He pledged himself to be their God and to make them his people. Moreover, this covenant was ratified with the blood of sacrifice: "Moses . . . took the blood, sprinkled it on the people and said, 'This is the blood of the covenant that the Lord has made with you in accordance with all these words'" [Exodus 24:8]. Hundreds of years passed, in which the people forsook God, broke his covenant and provoked his judgment.[4]

Throughout biblical history God, in his kindness, provided mediators for his people to represent them in making atonement for their sins and in renewing his covenants. Moses was one such mediator—but Moses was only human. We see his flesh-and-blood limitations reflected at Mount Sinai: Even Moses was shielded from God's presence by a thick cloud, and even Moses said, "I tremble with fear" (v. 21). God would graciously renew his blood covenant through Moses as mediator that day (see Exodus 24), but Moses was just as unable to keep the covenant as God's people were. Moses' fear of the Lord was also marred by sin.

We see ourselves in the Israelites. By nature, we are unable and unwilling to fear God as we ought, and our sin causes us to hide from him in guilt and shame rather than to come to him with our need. We forsake him for our own desires, as Israel did time and again, and consequently we provoke his wrath. We do not fear God in worshipful reverence and awe, and so we fear lesser things more than we should.

What hope was there for Israel, including its mediator, Moses? What hope is there for us?

The Mediator of a New Covenant

We have incredible hope, actually. And it all centers on these words from Hebrews 12: "But you have come to . . . Jesus, the mediator of a new covenant" (vv. 22, 24). What new covenant does this refer to? God's promise to give his people the desire and ability to worship him with the reverence and awe his glory deserves—his promise to place the fear of him within new hearts:

> For this is the covenant that I will make with the house of Israel after those days, declares the Lord: I will put my law within them, and I will write it on their hearts. And I will be their God, and

they shall be my people. . . . For I will forgive their iniquity, and I will remember their sin no more.

Jeremiah 31:33–34

True and lasting hope for fearful sinners—rebels who have exchanged the fear of God for lesser fears—is found in Jesus Christ. He fulfilled this promise by giving himself as the perfect sacrifice for sin and acting as the forever-mediator between God and man. He made this promise possible for us by willingly and obediently fearing God while he walked on earth (Matthew 17:5), living a life of holiness, and willingly and obediently fearing God through his death on the cross (Hebrews 12:1–2, 24). In Stott's words, "Through the shedding of Jesus' blood in death God was taking the initiative to establish a new pact or 'covenant' with his people, one of the greatest promises of which would be the forgiveness of sinners."[5]

Think about the mediator Jesus is: Like Moses, he was born as a baby in human flesh; unlike Moses, Jesus was the firstborn of all creation (Colossians 1:15), the divine Son of God who existed before time and humbled himself from his rightful heavenly throne to a lowly manger (Philippians 2:7). Like Moses, Jesus appeared before God's glory on a mountain; unlike Moses, Jesus was the image of God's glory on the mountain who heard his Father say, "This is my beloved Son, with whom I am well pleased." Like Moses, Jesus would draw near to the thick darkness where God was; but unlike with Moses, the darkness was the full wrath of his Father poured out on the cross as he bore in his body the sins of the world (1 Peter 2:24). Your sins, and mine.

And like the man Moses, Jesus would sacrifice and mediate on behalf of God's people; but unlike Moses, Jesus, the God-man, would lay down his own life, a once-for-all sacrifice of eternal significance, through the spilling of his own blood (Hebrews 7:27). And God accepted his perfect act of worship by raising him from the dead and seating him at his right hand (Hebrews 12:2):

> Therefore he is the mediator of a new covenant, so that those who are called may receive the promised eternal inheritance, since a death has occurred that redeems them from the transgressions committed under the first covenant.
>
> Hebrews 9:15

Jesus Christ is the sacrifice our sin requires and the mediator we most need. So God sent his Son to save us from the wrath our sinful fear deserves, to restore in our hearts a right fear of him, motivated not by law, but by love. He's the fulfillment of God's new-covenant promise of forgiveness that frees and grace that transforms:

> If you, O Lord, should mark iniquities,
> O Lord, who could stand?
> But with you there is forgiveness,
> *that you may be feared.*
> Psalm 130:3–4, emphasis added

Fear of Condemnation

Are you like the Israelites before Mount Sinai, trembling for fear of the consuming fire of God's judgment? Or have you trusted Jesus to take your judgment upon himself? Have you accepted his invitation to you, "Rise, and have no fear"? If you have, God's promise in Christ applies to you:

> There is therefore now no condemnation for those who are in Christ Jesus. For the law of the Spirit of life has set you free in Christ Jesus from the law of sin and death. . . . For you did not receive the spirit of slavery to fall back into fear, but you have received the Spirit of adoption as sons, by whom we cry, "Abba! Father!"
>
> Romans 8:1–2, 15

Some of you reading this have never received Jesus as your Savior and Lord, so you're living in rebellion against God and, as a result, under his wrath. I beg you not to stay there—come to Jesus. Recognize your lowliness before God, who provided his Son to save you from the wrath your sinful fear deserves and to restore in your heart a right fear of him. He's the only mediator of a new covenant: Jesus beckons you to rise and have no fear—to trust him as God's beloved Son who feared the Father perfectly in your place through his life and death. He invites you into the bright presence of God by offering himself as a living sacrifice for your sin and by spilling his blood for your forgiveness. When you trust him by faith, Jesus delights to serve you continually by placing his Spirit within you and by praying for you in heaven. Come to him, friend. Come to the only One who can bring you back to God.

Some of you reading this would say you're a Christian—but you toil within yourself at times, doubting this reality. Because you still sin, guilt weighs upon you. When the fear of condemnation looms, you wonder if God's promise of forgiveness is too good to be true.

But it's not—as God's beloved Son who pleased him perfectly on your behalf, Jesus accomplished for you what you never could. When your heart condemns you, he is greater than your heart (1 John 3:20), and you can remind yourself that there is no condemnation for those who are in him (Romans 8:1). When the enemy accuses you—one of his favorite tactics—remember the truth about Jesus that sets you free (John 8:31–32), that his perfect record of fearing God has become yours by faith.[6] And when you fail to fear God as you should and sin against him, confess to him, knowing he is faithful and just to forgive and cleanse you from all unrighteousness (1 John 1:9).

In Matthew Henry's words, "It is Christ by his word, and the power of his grace going along with it, that raises up good men from their dejections, and silences their fears; and none but Christ can do it."[7] And Christ has done it. He is the only Mediator and Savior who casts away the dark cloud of condemnation by his bright and glorious presence. So rise, and have no fear.

All Other Promises

Our passage in Hebrews ends with this encouragement: "Therefore let us be grateful for receiving a kingdom that cannot be shaken, and thus let us offer to God acceptable worship, with reverence and awe, for our God is a consuming fire" (Hebrews 12:28–29). Through Jesus Christ, God's consuming fire no longer threatens to destroy us, but promises to refine us. What God has done for our souls motivates us to please him, to offer him acceptable worship with reverence and awe—to fear him.

As we seek to fear Jesus in this life, we will face many other fears. In the remaining chapters, we will address these by looking at some of God's attributes and promises, all of which find their fulfillment—their yes and amen—in his Son (2 Corinthians 1:20).

LEARNING TO TRUST

PONDER. Memorize Romans 8:1: "There is therefore now no condemnation for those who are in Christ Jesus."

PRESERVE. Think about God's promise in Jeremiah 31 to forgive the iniquities of his people and remember their sin no more. How has he fulfilled this in his Son?

PREPARE. How will you respond when the fear of condemnation arises in you? Do you need to come to Jesus for the first time? Or do you need to remember Romans 8:1?

PRAY. *Almighty God, you are awesome and glorious. I have often hidden my face from you in guilt and shame. Through Christ, my Mediator, forgive all my iniquities and remember my sins no more! I trust in Jesus, your beloved Son, who pleased you fully so that I might be brought near to you again. O God, let me offer to you acceptable worship, with reverence and awe, for you are a consuming fire. In Jesus' name, amen.*

There is therefore now **no condemnation** *for those who are* in Christ Jesus.

ROMANS 8:1

God,
who is worthy
to be feared

three

I AM SOVEREIGN
(When You Fear Not Being in Control)

I am God, and there is no other;
I am God, and there is none like me,
declaring the end from the beginning
and from ancient times things not yet done,
saying, "My counsel shall stand,
and I will accomplish all my purpose."

Isaiah 46:9–10

LESLIE FEARS WHAT could happen to the baby she's carrying in her womb. Tom knows he cannot guarantee the well-being of his pregnant wife and their child and goes to sleep nervous every night. Jessica is always scared for her kids' safety, and Ron struggles with the fear of getting cancer. Brittany's anxiety feels out of her control, coming on full force at random moments, and she fears the next unexpected attack.

Then there are fears about natural disasters, such as devastating earthquakes and forest fires that can't be contained, and fears surrounding politics as people anxiously await the choices their leaders will make, choices that are out of their hands. And we fear tragedy, whether it's sudden harm coming to our family members or a seemingly random terrorist attack.

As finite creatures living in a world affected by sin, we fear anything out of our control. When I surveyed a group of people on social media, by far the most common response to the question "What do you most fear?" was a version of "things happening that I can't do anything about." We feel that we are not in control of people and plans, the present and the future—and the fruit of this feeling is *fear*.

The Umbrella

In the next two chapters, we'll address the fear of not being in control and another one like it, the fear that our worst fears will come to pass. We'll meditate on two attributes of God that speak to these fears—his sovereignty (that he is in control) and his goodness—and how they must always be held closely together:

- If we believe God is sovereign but not good, we'll wrongly view him as cold and malicious when we face hard circumstances.
- If we believe God is good but not sovereign, we'll struggle to trust his authority and his ability to change our circumstances.

- But as we believe that God is both sovereign and good, we'll grow in trusting him when we're afraid.

Picture an umbrella. God's sovereignty and goodness, among his many other attributes, are like the overarching top that encompasses the wires underneath. The six promises we'll look at in this book are like the wires: They're informed and held together by who God is, including his sovereignty and goodness.

Sovereignty and Goodness

We must first look at these two attributes of God to grasp what he intends by the promises he makes in his Word. Knowing God's character and his Word protects us from distorting and applying his promises apart from their biblical meaning. We must always handle God's precious words with care, interpreting Scripture in light of Scripture.[1]

For instance, take Romans 8:28: "And we know that for those who love God all things work together for good, for those who are called according to his purpose." It's easy to think this promise means that God will turn every bad and hard circumstance into something favorable, positive, and good. Though he certainly can and does do this for his people, God's promise of goodness here must be understood in light of all other truths about him, and especially his sovereign plan to make us like Jesus (see Romans 8:29). We'll look at this in more depth in the next chapter.

What Is the Sovereignty of God?

And so we dive into the first attribute: What does it mean that God is sovereign, and what does God's sovereignty mean for our fear of being out of control?

First, *God's sovereignty is his supreme authority and all-encompassing, wise rule over creation.* From Genesis to Revelation, Scripture reveals how God acts according to his will and purposes and is controlled by nothing and no one. Jerry Bridges defines God's sovereignty as "His absolute independence to do as He pleases and His absolute control over the actions of all His creatures."[2] God does what he wants, when he wants to, and how he wants to, and he has every right to exercise this control because he is God.

A.W. Tozer adds that "to be sovereign God must be all-knowing, all-powerful, and absolutely free."[3] God's perfect rule over his creation, then, involves his total knowledge of all things and his total power to exercise that knowledge in accordance with his purposes. This is the meaning of God's *wisdom*, which directs his perfect rule over his creation:

> The Lord *by wisdom* founded the earth;
> *by understanding* he established the heavens;
> *by his knowledge* the deeps broke open,
> and the clouds drop down the dew.
>
> Proverbs 3:19–20, emphasis added

What God's Sovereignty Is Not

To help us grasp what God's sovereignty is like, let's think about what it is *not* like. Some people hold to one extreme view, called *deism*, that God is like a clockmaker who set the world into motion but who now stands far off in observation. They believe he holds a type of creative power over the world, as the clockmaker does over his clocks, but isn't intimately involved in its happenings.

My husband and I recently watched a documentary about ocean life. I've been struck by God's creative and sovereign hand within the depths and the details of underwater ecosystems—such proof against deism's claims! Animals and plants I never knew existed are intimately known by God as their Creator and guided by him as their Sovereign. Not a sea urchin, not an orca, not a tidal wave or an ocean storm lives, moves, or has its being apart from his plan and purposes (Acts 17:28). Our God is that intimately involved in his creation—from the tiniest sea plankton to the expanse of the deep blue—wisely directing every atom of it toward his ends.

But does this mean we're robots? If deism is one extreme, then the opposite would be *determinism*. In this view, God's sovereignty negates our responsibility, making us robots who do only what he causes us to do. Determinism means human choice is nonexistent. But Scripture refutes both of these extreme views, emphasizing that humans are responsible actors *and* that God is sovereign. In Jerry Bridges's words, "God is able and does move upon the hearts and minds of people to accomplish His purposes. Yet . . . God does this without violating or coercing their wills, but rather that He works in His mysterious way *through* their wills to accomplish His purposes."[4] The two interweave in an incomprehensible display of God's mysterious ways.

Why We Fear Not Being in Control

In light of God's sovereignty, then, we need to ask a searching question: What's at the root of our fear of not being in control? Remember how sin corrupted our fear of the Lord, turning awe of God into terror before him, worship of God into idolatry, and reverence into rebellion against him. Our human predicament holds the answer to our question: We have rebelled against the only One who is in control, crowned ourselves as little sovereigns, and discovered we're terribly inadequate for the task. *We fear what we can't control because we have tried to control it but simply can't because we are not God.*[5]

This is not a new problem. In the Old Testament, we read of the Israelites falling prey again and again to this uneasy attempt at self-sovereignty as they try to take refuge from their enemies in other nations and in idols, instead of in their God. In Isaiah 46, Israel has been exiled to Babylon, and God compares himself to the idols worshiped in that place:

To whom will you liken me and make me equal,
    and compare me, that we may be alike?
Those who lavish gold from the purse,
    and weigh out silver in the scales,
hire a goldsmith, and he makes it into a god;
    then they fall down and worship!
They lift it to their shoulders, they carry it,
    they set it in its place, and it stands there;
    it cannot move from its place.
If one cries to it, it does not answer
    or save him from his trouble.

Isaiah 46:5–7

God describes Babylon's idols as dead and worthless substitutes for him, mere inanimate objects that have no control and can't save them from trouble. We may think, *Who in their right mind would think a statue could help them?* But we're more like Babylon than we'd like to admit:

We may not craft gold and silver into gods, but we do try to control our money for stability and power.

We may not fall down and worship statues, but we do worship ourselves and other people.

We may not cry out to an immovable object to save us from our troubles, but we do look to what we (think we) can control: people, possessions, and plans.

But in making idols of these things and trying to control what can't be controlled, we set ourselves up for fearfulness in times of inevitable trouble.

What God's Sovereignty Means for Our Fears

We see God's remedy for fearful and rebellious self-sovereigns in what he says next:

> Remember this and stand firm,
>> recall it to mind, you transgressors,
>> remember the former things of old;
> for I am God, and there is no other;
>> I am God, and there is none like me,
> declaring the end from the beginning
>> and from ancient times things not yet done,
> saying, "My counsel shall stand,
>> and I will accomplish all my purpose."
>
> Isaiah 46:8–10

God reminds Israel of his sovereign lordship that cannot and will not be surpassed. Babylon's gods can't move, let alone save, but our sovereign God moves, and has moved, according to his wisdom from before time, for the fulfillment of all his saving purposes—and because of who he is, we can trust him.

Throughout the book of Isaiah, this boundless wisdom and endless power are displayed as God unveils to his people his sovereign plan to save them, both historically from Babylonian captivity and eternally from the captivity of sin. He announces the coming of a Savior, One who would give up his heavenly crown to wear a crown of thorns, fulfilling God's sovereign plan of salvation for his people:

> Yet *it was the will of the Lord* to crush him;
>> he has put him to grief;

> when his soul makes an offering for guilt,
>> he shall see his offspring; he shall prolong his days;
>> *the will of the Lord* shall prosper in his hand.

Isaiah 53:10, emphasis added

So Jesus Christ came and lived and died and rose again, "according to the definite plan and foreknowledge of God" (Acts 2:23). The cross wasn't a random obstacle; it was a planned objective. God purposed his Son's work on the cross to bring sinners back to him and to restore in us a right fear of him as sovereign Lord over all things. And Jesus agreed with his Father's sovereign plan through joyful obedience. As John Stott so aptly says, "[Jesus] set his will to do his Father's will,"[6] and now "God has highly exalted [Jesus] and bestowed on him the name that is above every name, so that at the name of Jesus every knee should bow, in heaven and on earth and under the earth, and every tongue confess that Jesus Christ is Lord, to the glory of God the Father" (Philippians 2:9–11).

Because Jesus is Lord, we don't have to be. Because Christ is on his throne, ruling all things with perfect wisdom and power, we are freed from the crushing pressure and fearfulness of trying to rule ourselves, other people, and circumstances. As we learn of Jesus as our Savior *and* our Lord—that he's in control and that he's good—we will learn to trust and obey him in the circumstances that expose how out of control we are, including the following:

The Salvation of Loved Ones

No one can come to me unless the Father who sent me draws him.

John 6:44

Every Tuesday, I pray for friends and family who are far from God, that he would draw them near through faith in Christ. You and I are instruments of grace in God's hands; we are tools that he uses as we pray for the lost and share the good news about Jesus with them. We sow his Word, but salvation belongs to the Lord (Jonah 2:9). Because God is sovereign, we point people to Jesus with confidence that he can work through our witness, and because God is sovereign, we entrust people to Jesus with humility, knowing he holds the outcome in his hands.

People We Love

Your eyes saw my unformed substance;
in your book were written, every one of them,
the days that were formed for me,
when as yet there was none of them.

Psalm 139:16

One of our greatest fears is harm coming to the people we love, specifically losing them to tragedy. I battle this fear often as I think about my husband and our daughter. Yet our sovereign God created each of us with a specific number of days to fulfill (a truth we'll explore again in chapter 10). We can trust that God knows this number and that nothing will come to pass except what's written in his book.

The Future

Many are the plans in the mind of a man,
but it is the purpose of the Lord that will stand.

Proverbs 19:21

In a great and divine mystery, God's sovereignty and human plans work together to accomplish the purposes God has ordained for each of us. Such knowledge is too wonderful for us to grasp (Psalm 139:6), but this brings surety because a God we could fully grasp wouldn't be worthy of our fear. God's control over our futures also frees us to make decisions with confidence and comforts us over the outcomes of those decisions, especially when they seem confusing or don't go the way we had hoped.

Political Powers

> The king's heart is a stream of water in the hand of the Lord;
> he turns it wherever he will.
>
> Proverbs 21:1

God's guiding control over the hearts of his creation means we can trust political authorities into his sovereign hand and plans. Governing officials hold a degree of sovereign power, but only what has been entrusted to them by the only sovereign Lord. Nothing our authorities say or do is out of his control. Because of this, we can trust the King of kings and push back fear, even when earthly rulers disappoint and disparage us.

Nature

> He it is who makes the clouds rise at the end of the earth,
> who makes lightnings for the rain
> and brings forth the wind from his storehouses.
>
> Psalm 135:7

Even the wind and waves submit to their Creator, who can calm a storm by a command from his lips. Scripture says that God brings prosperity and disaster (Isaiah 45:7), and about this Jerry Bridges writes, "Whatever we experience at the hand of weather or other forces of nature . . . all circumstances are under the watchful eye and sovereign control of our God."[7]

Evil and Suffering

> The Lord has made everything for its purpose,
> even the wicked for the day of trouble.
>
> Proverbs 16:4

How does God's sovereignty intersect with the presence of evil, a cause of many of our fears? We'll look at this in more depth in chapter 6, but for now we'll end with this helpful truth from A.W. Tozer:

> In His sovereign wisdom God has permitted evil to exist in carefully restricted areas of His creation, a kind of fugitive outlaw whose activities are temporary and limited in scope. In doing this God has acted according to His infinite wisdom and goodness. More than that no one knows at present; and more than that no one needs to know.[8]

God's rule over evil is part of his plan, a reality that reaches far beyond our limited human understanding (Isaiah 55:9). Scripture is clear that God's own glory is his greatest end and highest goal (a topic for another book!), and that in his infinite wisdom God has determined that he'll receive the most glory through the limited activity of evil, along with all its effects, even sin and suffering.[9]

The problem of evil is complex, and while Scripture gives us some insight, at the end of the day our sovereign God calls us to trust him. Trusting him means we walk by faith, not by sight. It means we believe his sovereign wisdom is right and best, even when we can't make sense of it. It means that when we feel out of control, we find our rest in his perfect control:

> Clap your hands, all peoples!
>> Shout to God with loud songs of joy!
> For the Lord, the Most High, is to be feared,
>> a great king over all the earth.
>
> Psalm 47:1–2

LEARNING TO TRUST

PONDER. Memorize Isaiah 46:10: "My counsel shall stand, and I will accomplish all my purpose."

PRESERVE. Think about a time when you had a strong sense of God's sovereignty over and within your circumstances. How did this affect your fears? Have you seen his purposes at work in hindsight, even though you couldn't see them in the moment?

PREPARE. Which of the uncontrollable circumstances mentioned in this chapter do you fear most? What Scriptures can you take with you to wield as a sword of faith against those fears?

PRAY. *Sovereign God, you are perfect in power and wisdom. You are worthy to be feared and trusted. But you know I struggle with this. I put myself on your throne and try to control everything, and because of this, I'm afraid. Forgive my desire to be in control, and help me live in the freedom of your control. Help me bow at the name of Jesus, my Savior and Lord, even when I can't understand. Please free me from fear and fill me with joy through a deeper trust in your sovereignty. In Jesus' name, amen.*

My counsel shall stand, and *I* will accomplish all my purpose.

ISAIAH 46:10

four

I AM GOOD
(When You Fear the Worst)

Oh, taste and see that the Lord is good!
  Blessed is the man who takes refuge in him!
Oh, fear the Lord, you his saints,
  for those who fear him have no lack!
The young lions suffer want and hunger;
  but those who seek the Lord lack no good thing.

Psalm 34:8–10

TWENTY-FIVE YEARS AGO, my two brothers-in-law were successively diagnosed with leukemia. When Beth Wetherell got the news about her infant boy, she was shocked and devastated—and then a phone call came two weeks later, diagnosing her four-year-old son with the same type of cancer. She tells the story of that awful day in her memoir, *Our Help: Four Young Children, Two with Cancer, One Magnificent Promise*:

> "Mrs. Wetherell, this is Dr. Betti. I have the results. I believe Matthew has what Davis has. I believe Matthew has leukemia, too."
>
> A cold shiver ran through me.
>
> "No, Dr. Betti, you can't be telling me this," I said, rejecting his diagnosis.
>
> "I'm so sorry, Beth. In all my 30 years of practice, I have never seen this before."
>
> Silence. I began to unravel, unable to speak. How does your world stop . . . again?[1]

I try to put myself in my mother-in-law's shoes, try to imagine getting such a tragic call, and even the thought of it is unbearable. Running through my mind are people with stories of family and friends who've passed away from incurable diseases, neighbors who've lost loved ones to car accidents, mothers who've birthed stillborn babies, and kids who've been diagnosed with cancer, as Matt and Davis were.

Awful things can happen—they *do* happen—and we're terrified that they will happen to us. It's only a slight comfort to think that the odds of such tragedies are slim because we know, deep down in our hearts, that the realization of our worst fears could be just a phone call away.

God Is Good?

In the previous chapter, we investigated the sovereignty of God and how it speaks to our fear of not being in control. We saw how God's sovereignty must be held closely together with his goodness, that his attributes form a sort of umbrella top that encompasses the wires underneath (his promises). In this chapter, we will look at the second attribute, God's goodness, and how we can learn to trust God when we're afraid of the worst coming to pass.

Grappling with God's Goodness

"God is good" is a common Christian saying, but do we really believe this when the rubber hits the road? When the phone rings and the awful news arrives and our worst fears are realized—when *bad* things happen—can we still say with confidence that God is indeed good? This is a major challenge for the human heart as we hold in tension Scripture's witness that God is always good and the reality of suffering in a broken world. One of our fears is that this tension will become unavoidable: The rubber of our faith will hit the road of our circumstances, and we will have to wrestle by experience with a truth we've always said we believed.

Years ago I grappled with the constant fear of my Lyme disease flaring up and of the sudden injuries that could come from a body left weak from its destruction. It had taken six years and eight specialists to be properly diagnosed, and at that point much damage was done. As thankful as I was to have an answer to my health problems, I wrestled with what the future might hold: *Will I ever be healed from Lyme? Will I get my energy back, or will chronic fatigue be my new normal? Will I be able to have children? Will I generally be sick for the rest of my earthly life?*

I knew I wasn't dealing well with these fears when I began to see worry, bitterness, and doubt rising up within me. These undesirable and destructive attitudes often point to a heart that is wrestling with God's goodness. Have you seen them within yourself?

Worry

When we worry, we often fret about a future we have no control over, and we forget about the God who controls the future, a good God who says he desires to give us good things (Matthew 7:11). We picture a possibility and turn it into a probability—and our fear increases as a result. Sometimes, we truly want to stop worrying but find we can't. And in the most extreme cases, worry devolves into anxiety and panic.[2]

Bitterness

It is normal to question why bad things happen to good people while evil people seem to prosper, but we must be careful. Our seemingly innocent questions are insidious and can become accusations against God. Asaph, the author of Psalm 73, describes a time he fell into this dangerous place when he writes,

> But as for me, my feet had almost stumbled,
>   my steps had nearly slipped.
> For I was envious of the arrogant
>   when I saw the prosperity of the wicked. . . .
> When my soul was embittered,
>   when I was pricked in heart,
> I was brutish and ignorant;
>   I was like a beast toward you.
>
> vv. 2–3, 21–22

When a sense of entitlement stokes our fears, and we believe we deserve something better or different, the result is often a more consuming fearfulness. For if we start to believe that God's heart and intentions are not good toward us, and we accuse him of acting other than good, whom will we have to run to when future fears come to pass?

Doubt

When left unchecked, attitudes of worry and bitterness can lead to doubt, which is just another word for fearfulness or distrust.[3] In a culture that tells us to follow our heart and instincts, it's much easier to let our feelings rule us rather than our faith—but the result is an unanchored and unsteady heart that is easily shaken by circumstances: "The one who doubts is like a wave of the sea that is driven and tossed by the wind" (James 1:6). Doubt allows fear to grow in its unruly power, but faith chooses to overwhelm it with truth.

If you've noticed these attitudes within yourself, you're probably grappling with the goodness of God. When we can't seem to reconcile a good God with bad circumstances, it takes a toll on our trust in him. Of course, we can be proactive and shield ourselves with the truth of God's Word. Still, many fears catch us off guard and startle us with their power. For those of us struggling with the assurance that God is good because hard and bad times have already come, God invites us to his Word.

Psalm 34's Guide to Fighting Fear with God's Goodness

King David authored this beautiful poem. It is all about God's goodness, and its carefully crafted acrostic style displays the expanse of this goodness as David takes us through the Hebrew alphabet—sort of an "A to Z" of the benevolent nature of our God. David was certainly a blessed man who knew many good gifts from God's hand, but he was equally a hard-pressed man. God ordained many grueling trials throughout David's lifetime, and he endured such terrible darkness that he wrote of it as "the valley of the shadow of death" (Psalm 23:4):

- Unrelenting hatred and violent persecution by King Saul that forced David into hiding and placed him on the brink of death multiple times
- The betrayal of his son Absalom, who scorned him, attempted to steal his throne, and murdered many people David loved, including one of his other sons
- The death of his baby boy, a consequence of his adulterous affair with Bathsheba and the calculated murder of her husband
- A nation—God's chosen and precious nation—torn in two because of political strife and familial turmoil

No doubt, David wrestled with the goodness of God; we have proof of this in many of his psalms (see Psalms 68–70). But when the trials hit and the shadow of death enveloped him, David relied on what he knew, without a doubt, to be absolutely and always true: *God is good.* Don't you want such confidence? Don't you want to dampen the worry, bitterness, and doubt that so often stir up the flames of your fears? And what if they come to pass? Don't you want a sure and steady faith that God is still good?

We can fight our fears with God's truth, and David gives us a guide in this psalm. Let's learn from his words, which God has provided for us, that we might also learn to trust him:

Fight fear with praise

For a man who's exhausted, distressed, and wrestling with fear, David begins at an unlikely place. Despite his circumstances—indeed, in the middle of them—he chooses to praise God:

> I will bless the Lord at all times;
>> his praise shall continually be in my mouth. . . .
> Oh, magnify the Lord with me,
>> and let us exalt his name together!
>
> Psalm 34:1, 3

David has God's goodness in mind here, his benevolent heart that informs all he is and motivates all he does. His goodness runs behind and beneath his love and justice, his mercy and grace, his forgiveness and faithfulness, his patience and kindness. J. I. Packer elaborates:

> God's truthfulness and trustworthiness, his unfailing justice and wisdom, his tenderness, forbearance and entire adequacy to all who penitently seek his help, his noble kindness in offering believers the exalted destiny of fellowship with him in holiness and love—these things together make up God's goodness in the overall sense of the sum total of his revealed excellences.[4]

David knows that God is good and worthy to be feared, regardless of circumstances. He encourages us to fear God along with him by praising him "at all times" and "continually," a practice that will ready the quenching waters of truth for when the fire of our worst fears is set ablaze. For the more we praise him, the more we'll be prepared to praise him, even when fearful times come and it feels like a sacrifice: "Through [Jesus] then let us continually offer up a sacrifice of praise to God, that is, the fruit of lips that acknowledge his name" (Hebrews 13:15).

Fight fear with remembrance

Next, David reflects on a recent fearful dilemma, in which he was trapped by an enemy and pretended to be insane to escape from his grip (see 1 Samuel 21). He recounts God's goodness in rescuing him:

> This poor man cried, and the Lord heard him
> and saved him out of all his troubles.
> The angel of the Lord encamps
> around those who fear him, and delivers them.
>
> Psalm 34:6–7

The conscious act of remembering God's faithfulness to us in our past will deepen our trust in his present goodness, like it did for David. Scripture is full of God's commands that his people remember his works (Exodus 13:3; Deuteronomy 5:15; Isaiah 63:7), for this is faith strengthening and fear expelling. When you're wrestling with fear, think about his faithfulness: What prayers has God answered in your past? From what troubles has he saved you? What fears has he helped you overcome, even if by degrees? How have you recognized his goodness in hindsight?

Fight fear with perspective

David brings his poem to a climax with a declaration about God's goodness and an exhortation to God's people:

> Oh, taste and see that the Lord is good!
> Blessed is the man who takes refuge in him!
> Oh, fear the Lord, you his saints,
> for those who fear him have no lack!
> The young lions suffer want and hunger;
> but those who seek the Lord lack no good thing.
>
> Psalm 34:8–10

When we wrestle with God's goodness, it's often because he's taken, changed, or withheld something we think we need or deserve. I want to be especially sensitive here, as many of you have known incredible loss—your worst fears realized—and I can't pretend to understand the wrestling that comes with such pain. In any degree of our sufferings, whether seemingly small or life altering, God's Word here in Psalm 34:8–10 applies: *Those who fear him lack nothing. Those who fear him have every good thing.* With Christ, even in losing something good, we lack nothing. With Christ, even in gaining something bad, we have every good thing.

But how can this be? Three Scriptures from Romans 8 give us insight into this paradox.

Romans 8:28: The Good of Sanctification

We mentioned this verse briefly in the last chapter. It's a common one (sometimes poorly) cited when bad and fearful things happen: "And we know that for those who love God all things work together for good, for those who are called according to his purpose." The apostle Paul, who wrote Romans, isn't saying that all our circumstances will work themselves out, but that God will be at work within us—sanctifying us—through every circumstance. This sanctifying work he's doing is *good*, conforming us to the holiness of Jesus: "For those whom he foreknew he also predestined to be conformed to the image of his Son" (Romans 8:29). In Sam Alberry's words, "God is not working all things so that this life will be one of financial riches, good health, or popularity. God is working all things so that we will become *more and more like his Son*."[5]

Those who seek the Lord lack no good thing, including becoming holy as Jesus is holy.

Romans 8:32: The Good of Spiritual Blessings

"He who did not spare his own Son but gave him up for us all, how will he not also with him graciously give us all things?" (Romans 8:32). Again, "all things" doesn't necessarily mean earthly benefits. Rather, earthly pains and losses are meant to stir our longing for heavenly blessings and gains (Romans 8:19), all of which God has given us through his Son: justification, new-creation life, adoption as sons and daughters, sanctification by his Spirit, and the assurance of our future heavenly home, which is as sure as the cross-work of Christ is finished. "Paul is telling us that there is no ultimate loss or irreparable impoverishment to be feared; if God denies us something, it is only in order to make room for one or other of the things he has in mind," writes Packer.[6]

One particular spiritual blessing that has helped me fight fear is the gift of God's grace. *Grace* refers to God's unmerited favor, and it includes all the blessings this favor entails, what Ephesians 1:7 calls "the riches of his grace." Christian, God has graciously given you all these things:

- Strength and power (Acts 6:8; 2 Corinthians 12:9)
- Hope (Romans 5:2)
- Righteousness (Romans 5:21)
- Peace (2 Corinthians 1:2; Galatians 1:3)
- Provision (2 Corinthians 8:6–7)
- Sufficiency (2 Corinthians 9:8)
- Wisdom (Ephesians 1:8)
- Truth (Colossians 1:5–7)
- Comfort (2 Thessalonians 2:16)
- Love (1 Timothy 1:14)
- Help (Hebrews 4:16)

You may not *feel* all these blessings all the time, but rest assured they are yours in the grace of our Lord Jesus Christ. Grace, in all its riches, sustains and strengthens us in the fight of faith, just as manna sustained and strengthened the Israelites in the wilderness. God gave them "a day's portion every day" (Exodus 16:4), just the amount they needed. And God promises to give us what we need for *today*. As a wise friend recently said to me, "God doesn't give tomorrow's grace today." Fear comes when we envision tomorrow's circumstances apart from tomorrow's grace. But trust deepens as we focus on God's favor toward us *today*—his promise to give us spiritual blessings for the moment—and as we leave the future, along with its needed grace, in his good hands.

Those who seek the Lord lack no good thing, including every spiritual blessing.

Romans 8:38–39: The Good of Tasting and Seeing Jesus

Finally, the apostle Paul writes this with triumphant confidence: "For I am sure that neither death nor life, nor angels nor rulers, nor things present nor things to come, nor powers, nor height nor depth, nor anything else in all creation, will be able to separate us from the love of God in Christ Jesus our Lord." Our trust in God's goodness will deepen as we taste and see that his greatest gift, Jesus Christ, can never be lost or taken from us, even when earthly gifts are. We fight our fears with an even greater fear, the fear of the Lord, as gaining Jesus becomes more precious to us than anything we might lose.

Those who seek the Lord lack no good thing, including, and ultimately, the Lord himself.

Taste and See

When our worst fears come to pass (or we're afraid that they will), our trust in God's goodness will deepen as we "taste and see" Jesus' fellowship with us in suffering: his agony that produced bloody sweat as he anticipated drinking the cup of God's wrath on the cross where he became sin for us, tasting death in our place. Our trust in God's goodness will also deepen as we taste and see the power of Jesus' resurrection as he overcame death, that we might never taste death ourselves but dwell in his saving love and eternal life. J. I. Packer points us to the cross when he says, "Calvary is the measure of the goodness of God."[7]

Paul gives us a similar perspective in Philippians 3:7–8: "But whatever gain I had, I counted as loss for the sake of Christ. Indeed, I count everything as loss because of the surpassing worth of knowing Christ Jesus my Lord." *Jesus*, he writes, *is better to me than anything. Even the greatest earthly loss is gain if it means knowing Jesus more as a result; and even the greatest earthly gain is loss compared to knowing and trusting him.*

Can we say the same?

My mother-in-law also attests to this, not only because her two boys survived their battle with cancer, but because God is always, always good, even when the worst happens:

> My faith in the Gospel was not tested by the deaths of my sons, but I've known others who have endured just such a test and have still found God to be all He promised. [My dear friend's] . . . teen nephew passed away from leukemia a few years ago. Matthew's parents are Christians, and so was Matthew . . . if you were to talk with this young man's mom and dad, they would still be a witness to our true God and could share the many ways God has been their help in the midst of much sorrow. . . . This is why so many Christians can say with confidence, "It is well with my soul," no matter what trial or circumstance they face. They know the bottom line: God can be trusted.[8]

LEARNING TO TRUST

PONDER. Memorize Psalm 34:10: "The young lions suffer want and hunger; but those who seek the Lord lack no good thing."

PRESERVE. Think through the questions under the "Fight Fear with Remembrance" section earlier in this chapter.

PREPARE. Knowing that one of God's spiritual blessings in Christ is grace for the moment, how does this truth strengthen you to fight fear and face the future with confidence in him?

PRAY. *Gracious God, you are always good. Open my eyes to see your goodness, most evident in the giving of your Son for my salvation. Help me to see all my circumstances in light of this ultimate act of your goodness. And forgive me when I haven't had your perspective, when I've thought you unkind, even cruel, and have given my heart to worry, bitterness, and doubt. I want to taste and see that you are good! I want to take refuge in you, even when the worst storms come my way. Help me push back fear by trusting in your goodness, and in your all-sufficient grace, more and more. In Jesus' name, amen.*

The young lions
suffer want and hunger;
but those who seek the Lord
lack no good thing.

PSALM 34:10

God's precious and very great promises

five

I WILL PROVIDE
(When You Fear You Won't Have Enough)

*And do not seek what you are to eat and what you are to drink,
nor be worried. For all the nations of the world seek after these
things, and your Father knows that you need them. Instead,
seek his kingdom, and these things will be added to you.*

*Fear not, little flock, for it is your Father's good pleasure to
give you the kingdom.*

Luke 12:29–32

THEY FOUND MORE asbestos. I don't know what we're
going to do."

My husband and I had just closed on our first home, a one-level
ranch built in 1970, and we were preparing to move. Nothing had
financially stretched us more than this purchase; we had saved for

years and thanked God for providing us a home near our church, where my husband had been called as a pastor. Everything had seemed fine with the house before closing, so we approached the day with excited nerves—until a flooring contractor broke the news that a sample from the original tile had revealed asbestos, a dormant carcinogen made hazardous when disturbed. This news meant unexpected hassle and costs, and we were obviously frustrated. But at least we found the problem *before* closing, and we could compromise with the seller to deal with it.

Or so we thought.

Now, postclosing and a week away from our hoped-for move, my husband had more news to share: Our house's air ducts, an unreachable system located in the concrete slab under the house, were made from asbestos. If we wanted to breathe clean air, we'd not only have to abate the toxic material, we'd have to seal off the old ducts with cement and install a new attic system.

We had not planned for this. And we were terrified.

Lying in bed that night, I wondered why God had led us to that house, why he'd let us close on it, when we'd prayed for guidance and protection. I was three months pregnant at the time and feeling (especially) emotional and afraid. My head was spinning. *How are we possibly going to pay for the construction, let alone make ends meet after this? How did we get in this situation, and how will we get out of it?*

By God's grace, and only by his grace, we did.

Two years later, I sit here in the living room of our home, and I see how God has provided for us—not always in ways we expected, but always in the right and best way. We saw him answer our desperate prayers for financial help, yes—but what strikes me most is that God answered our original prayer: He *did* protect our family (from the harms of asbestos), and he *did* guide us (through many hard decisions and tasks). More than all of this, he exercised our trust in his ability and willingness to give us what we most needed.

We worried, and we were anxious. But God provided, in more ways than one.

The Fear of Not Having Enough

Just as my husband and I were sweating with panic when we heard about our noxious air duct system (not to mention after our washer and dryer *and* water heater broke immediately upon our moving in), have you ever found yourself in a financial emergency? Or are you, right this moment, afraid of not having what you need today? The fear of not having enough is most often connected to money and material possessions, though we should also consider two more resources we're afraid to lack: capacity and time.

Let's look more closely at each of these three categories.

Lack of money and possessions

We live in the United States, so I'm writing this from a particular cultural perspective. Ours is one of the wealthiest nations on earth, yet it seems we are also the most anxious: We worry about our bank accounts, the stock market, and our retirement nest eggs. We worry about job security and our kids' futures. We worry about inflation as gas prices and food costs and insurance fees increase. And have you ever found it odd that Americans celebrate special days based solely on money and possessions, such as Black Friday and Cyber Monday? We also treasure freedom of choice and boast of endless options; just take a walk down the bread aisle at the grocery store, or around the car dealership lot. The purchasing possibilities are overwhelming.

We place so much of our personal value and peace of mind on financial stability that anxiety often drives our decision-making. When money and possessions slip away, or there's a chance of them slipping away, we grow troubled and anxious. We're either obsessed with gaining more and more, always seeking the next best thing, or we're stingy, saving up and storing away for rainy days.

We're the nation that seems to have everything—yet we're continually afraid of not having enough.

Recently, I read an insightful article on a financial website written by its founder, a man who grew up in poverty. What he says about fear is striking:

> I have dreaded the thought of ever returning to a state of anything close to poverty. I don't want my children to ever feel as though their parents were anything less than reliable. I don't want to ever feel like tomorrow will bring complete uncertainty into my life.
>
> It's a deep fear and a painful one. It's driven me to make some less-than-productive choices over the years. It's caused me to work way too hard at various points, pushing myself into illness with the stress. It convinced me to dig so deep into frugality that I began to turn into a cheapskate.
>
> Yet, even after all of that, the fear is still there. I don't know that the fear of poverty will ever really truly and completely go away.[1]

Many of us know this fear, the uncertainty of tomorrow. We get it, even though most of us haven't grown up in poverty. The fear of not having enough money (or the stuff money can buy) stresses us out and keeps us awake at night.

Lack of time

Closely tied to our American consumer culture is the American spirit. Ambitious and tireless personalities win, hard work earns rewards, busyness is a virtue, and the strong and gifted climb the ladder. But time off? Slowing down? Sleep? *Time's running out,* we silently fret. How often do we fear we won't have enough of it? Time to finish our work, be with our families, serve other people, rest. Rather than embrace twenty-four-hour days with vigor, intentionality, and gratitude to their Creator, we fear them and worry about the day ahead before it even begins.

And we Americans are terrible receivers of God's gift of rest; we often refuse it for fear of getting behind and losing ground. So we work ourselves to the bone and wring out of our day all the seconds we can, to the detriment of our bodies and souls.

Lack of capacity

We also fear anything that reveals how limited and weak we truly are. It's a common belief that human weakness is a result of the fall, but God actually created us with weaknesses and limitations. We were never meant to be all-powerful, infinite, and self-sufficient like God is. Some of you, however, know unique limitations such as chronic pain and illness that *are* a result of sin's effect on creation. These acute weaknesses keep you from doing what you had always hoped you'd do. Others have injuries or diseases that may never heal in this life, and you know what it is to worry about what abilities you will have tomorrow.

Our God stands infinitely apart from us in this way. He has no needs and no lack. Jen Wilkin says it well: "Our God is . . . needed by all, needful of nothing."[2] But sin, and the rebellion that sin fosters, resists the fact that we aren't him. All of us want to be like God (Genesis 3:5), yet we simply can't be, and we fear whatever circumstances expose this reality.

All These Things Will Be Added to You

We recognize these fears within the American spirit and culture, but they aren't limited to us—they're deeply ingrained within the *human* spirit. Autonomous, consumer cultures seem to heighten them, but you don't need to live in America to fear the things we fear. When sin distorted our fear of God and twisted the way we think about him, the whole human race stopped trusting his sovereign control and his good heart. Instead, we suspect that God is holding out on us and that we must provide for ourselves. Enter anxiety and worry and fear. But Jesus knew this about the human heart, and he addresses this universal fear with a promise:

> And do not seek what you are to eat and what you are to drink, nor be worried. For all the nations of the world seek after these things, and your Father knows that you need them. *Instead, seek his kingdom, and these things will be added to you.* Fear not, little flock, for it is your Father's good pleasure to give you the kingdom.
>
> Luke 12:29–32, emphasis added

Before we can grasp what Jesus means here, we should look at three things he doesn't mean.

First, Jesus can't mean that his people will never experience poverty. He did himself, and his people often do.[3] Second, Jesus doesn't mean that God will bless us with material things if we seek him, as though he's a cosmic genie or vending machine: good deeds in, good blessings out. That's prosperity theology, and it's a far cry from what God's Word says about the cost of following him.[4] Lastly, when Jesus says, "Do not seek what you are to eat and what you are to drink," he doesn't mean it's wrong to seek our daily necessities. God created us to depend on these basic provisions, and we should pursue them in God-honoring ways.

Rather, Jesus is saying, "Do not *only* seek these things—do not let these things be the reason for your existence—there's a greater, more important thing to seek." He's comparing the world's pursuits—wealth, possessions, and earthly treasures—to the pursuit of lasting treasure in God's kingdom, and the greatest Treasure—himself. He encourages us to *look beyond* the temporal needs of the body to the eternal needs of our soul.

But how? What, then, does God's promise mean?

The Provision of God's Care

For all the nations of the world seek after these things, and your Father knows that you need them.

Luke 12:30

Remember how our Creator is not aloof, but sovereignly involved in his creation. He's active and generous toward all he has made. While God isn't obligated to provide anything for us, his good heart and sovereign hand give us far more than we deserve on a daily basis. His common grace extends to all—even the ravens (v. 24) and the lilies (v. 27)—as he opens his hand to give creation what it needs (Psalm 145:16).

Yet God cares about his people even more than he cares about birds and flowers.

Notice in this passage how Jesus says "your Father" twice. God's fatherly promise to care for his children is intimate, unchanging, and motivated by love—the epitome of an earthly mom and dad's care for their kids. God has our best in mind, and when we are afraid of not having enough, we can return to his promise that those who seek him lack no good thing. Matthew Henry writes, "God, who has done the greater for us [saving our souls], may be depended upon to do the less [sustaining our bodies]."[5] John Flavel agrees when he writes, "Will we trust Him for heaven and not for earth?"[6]

As we learn to trust God's heart, we'll learn to trust his hand. God won't necessarily give us everything we want or think we need, but everything he knows we most need. And we can trust his sovereign, good heart—in abundance or lack, ease or hardship— because he has already provided for our greatest need in Christ.

The Provision of God's Kingdom

Instead, seek his kingdom, and these things will be added to you.

Luke 12:31

When we're afraid we won't have enough, we need to be reminded of all we've been given in Jesus Christ: the grace of repentance, forgiveness of our sins, righteous standing before God, adoption as God's children, the indwelling of his Spirit, a place at his heavenly table, and all the riches of our inheritance in God's kingdom—his eternal heavenly reality. And this is not an exhaustive list; everything that is Christ's becomes ours when we're united to him by faith (1 Corinthians 3:21–22). Through him, we are rich in every way that truly and eternally matters:

> According to [God's] great mercy, he has caused us to be born again to a living hope through the resurrection of Jesus Christ from the dead, to an inheritance that is imperishable, undefiled, and unfading, kept in heaven for you, who by God's power are being guarded through faith for a salvation ready to be revealed in the last time.
>
> 1 Peter 1:3–5

That God delights to give us such an undeserved gift in his Son motivates us to seek his kingdom with all our hearts, to make it our primary pursuit, to "press on to make it [our] own, because Christ Jesus has made [us] his own" (Philippians 3:12). Fears that our temporal, time-bound needs may not be met are put in their proper perspective in light of our eternal need that has already been met. And God's promise is true: His lasting provision for us in his kingdom includes adding to us our daily bread, and *infinitely more*: "And my God will supply every need of yours according to his riches in glory in Christ Jesus" (Philippians 4:19).

The Provision of God's Son

> Fear not, little flock, for it is your Father's good pleasure to give you the kingdom.
>
> Luke 12:32

Jesus' mission on earth was to seek God's kingdom without wavering and make it a reality for God's people. But for Jesus to seek and find all the riches of the kingdom, he would have to become poor. For Jesus to take his place at his Father's right hand in glory, he would have to leave it and become a servant with no earthly place to lay his head. For Jesus to gather his flock, he would have to become the sacrificial lamb. For Jesus to become the incomparable and priceless treasure of all those he would save, he would have to pay the price with his own blood:

> For you know the grace of our Lord Jesus Christ, that though he was rich, yet for your sake he became poor, so that you by his poverty might become rich.
>
> 2 Corinthians 8:9

The kingdom is only desirable and glorious because of the King. More than we seek his gifts, as good and needed as they are, we seek him, the Giver, who is infinitely worthy to be trusted and feared. Our greatest treasure is him, "the light of the knowledge of the glory of God in the face of Jesus Christ" (2 Corinthians 4:6), which we carry in temporal "jars of clay, to show that the surpassing power belongs to God and not to us" (v. 7). The more we learn to treasure Jesus, the less we will treasure the world. And the less we treasure the world, the less we will fear what we may not have in it, as we consider Jesus all-sufficient—always enough—for us.

Two Applications to Fight Your Fears

Let's look now at a couple of applications that will help loosen our grip on the earthly treasures of money and possessions, time, and capacity and therefore loosen the grip of fear. We find these woven throughout the other parts of Luke 12:

Fight your fears over a lack of money and possessions by giving generously.

Sell your possessions, and give to the needy. Provide yourselves with moneybags that do not grow old, with a treasure in the heavens that does not fail.

Luke 12:33

Train your heart to treasure Christ and his kingdom by investing in it, and loosen your hold on money and possessions by giving them away. Give to your local church, missionaries, and people in need through financial donations, prayer, and service. Ask God to help you remember that all you have been entrusted with belongs to him, and ask for a heart to give it back to him with joy and trust in his ability to provide for you.

Fight your fears over a lack of time and capacity by spending your life wisely.

Stay dressed for action and keep your lamps burning, and be like men who are waiting for their master to come home from the wedding feast, so that they may open the door to him at once when he comes and knocks. Blessed are those servants whom the master finds awake when he comes.

Luke 12:35–37

Wise use of our time and capacity means living with eternity in mind. As a Christian, you are not living for yourself—you are living for Christ (2 Corinthians 5:15). Life is short, and eternity is long; you want to live with that perspective, knowing Jesus is coming back. So ask yourself often, "Am I spending my days in service to my King? Am I using the opportunities, relationships, and gifts he's given me, even my weaknesses, for the sake of his name?" When you can say yes, you'll know you are using your time and capacities well, and your anxiety over limitations will diminish.

LEARNING TO TRUST

PONDER. Memorize Luke 12:32: "Fear not, little flock, for it is your Father's good pleasure to give you the kingdom."

PRESERVE. How have you seen God provide for you (and others) in the past, whether financially or by increasing your time or physical capacity?

PREPARE. Put into action the section "Two Applications to Fight Your Fears."

PRAY. *King Jesus, you are my greatest treasure. Because I have you, I am truly rich. I want to trust that you are all-sufficient for me. Strengthen me, by the help of your Spirit, to seek your kingdom above all other pursuits. Show me how you are caring for me on a daily basis, and remind me of your care for my soul. Show me that I can trust your hand as I trust your heart. Amen.*

Fear not, little flock, for it is your Father's *good pleasure* to give you the kingdom.

LUKE 12:32

I WILL PROTECT YOU

(When You Fear Evil)

The Lord is your keeper;
the Lord is your shade on your right hand.
The sun shall not strike you by day,
nor the moon by night.
The Lord will keep you from all evil;
he will keep your life.
The Lord will keep
your going out and your coming in
from this time forth and forevermore.

Psalm 121:5–8

P LEASE DON'T SHOOT. Please don't shoot...."
I kept repeating those three desperate words. Moments earlier, my friend and I had been finishing our conversation in

my car when a masked figure appeared at her window, holding a gun. Now he pointed the weapon at my friend's chest and told us to give him our stuff.

Fear pulsed through me. All I could think was, *I don't want to die.* "Don't shoot," I continued to plead, hoping he would have mercy. Then he told my friend to get out of the car.

She obeyed, her eyes fixed on the gun aimed at her. Carefully, she opened her door and stepped out, while I sat paralyzed in the driver's seat. Moments passed as my friend dug around her purse for anything of value, anything to appease his demands and spare us harm. And it worked; after she surrendered her wallet and phone, we heard the eight words that saved our lives: "Get back in the car, and drive away."

Our narrow escape in the dark of the night is a vague memory, but soon we were in a parking lot dialing 911 and campus police to report the armed robbery. We were sobbing and in shock. All our valuables were gone.

But we were alive. Praise be to God, alive.

I don't remember much about that night, but I do remember one thing clearly: *the fear.* The white-hot fear. To this day, I'm thankful that this frightening episode didn't cause post-traumatic stress disorder or a resistance to driving at night. Sometimes I forget it even happened—it seems like a nightmare, or a scene from a movie, but not real life.

The Reality of Evil

Since that night, however, I've become more aware of the reality of evil. Adulthood will do this. I look at our world and see acts of terrorism, public shootings, and brutal murders, and all of these make me afraid. When I'm in confined public places, I'm usually plotting my escape route, and at night before bed, I form a plan in case an intruder breaks in. I suppose some of this is wisdom, but the temptation is for me to become paralyzed by these fears, to refuse to go to concerts or fly in an airplane or visit an indoor mall.

Evil is a fearful thing. The world is not as it should be. When human life, our most treasured earthly possession, is threatened, of course we're going to react, self-protect, and avoid dangerous situations. This is God's gift of natural, merciful fear at work. There's a commonsense element to this, and we shouldn't disregard evil or pretend it doesn't exist.

But there's a fine line between common sense and paralyzation, the type that keeps us from living our lives because of an unhealthy focus on any fear, past, present, or future—of a hypothetical threat or a real one. How do we fight this kind of paralyzing fear of evil?

God, Your Keeper

Psalm 121 gives us a starting point. It describes an ascent to Jerusalem, a long trek to worship God in his holy temple, when his people would have encountered a scorching sun, uneven paths, and the possibility of robbers along the way—many reasons to fear the long journey. With these dangers in view, the psalmist sings:

> I lift up my eyes to the hills.
>   From where does my help come?

> My help comes from the Lord,
>> who made heaven and earth.
>>> vv. 1–2

I will keep my eyes on the hills. The psalmist looks to the highest peak of the mountain and is reminded of God's greatness. The hills are fixed, a picture of the immovable Creator, the One who formed them with a word and who could remove them—and every present danger—in an instant. Then the psalmist exhorts God's people with a promise:

> The Lord will keep you from all evil;
>> he will keep your life.
> The Lord will keep
>> your going out and your coming in
>> from this time forth and forevermore.
>>> vv. 7–8

The psalm's author isn't named, but if the writer was David, remember his experience. He had a ruthless enemy, King Saul, who tried to take his life multiple times. As king, David rarely knew peace as foreign nations declared war on Israel throughout the majority of his reign. He also had beloved family members betray him and seek his downfall. David knew evil's presence intimately, yet he could still declare this wonderful promise in Psalm 121: "The Lord will keep you from all evil."

The word *keep* has special significance here. Throughout this passage, it could be replaced with the words *protect* or *guard*: "The Lord will protect you from all evil. The Lord will guard your life."

What an incredible promise—and, at times, a confusing one. So what are we to make of it? How do we understand God's promise of protection when we see evidence of evil every day, when it appears to us that God's people aren't always protected from it?

God's Protecting Power

This is a question I've wrestled with for a long time. *If God says he'll protect me, does that mean nothing bad will happen?* I think about the believers who were worshiping God at a church in Texas, only to be visited by a gunman, or those gathered in South Carolina for a prayer meeting who were murdered by a white supremacist. *What about them, God? You didn't protect them. . . .* And what about my cousin's friend, whose husband was murdered by an intruder one night while they were sleeping? Where was God's protection then?

My struggle with this has given fear the advantage at times. I'm not sure when I last went to bed without thought of someone harming our family. No, this fear hasn't stopped me from living, but it has stifled me from trusting—and I so badly want to believe God when he says he'll protect me.

But what exactly does his promise mean? If evil happens to God's people, in what ways does he protect us?

God protects his creatures from harm.

God's promise can't mean that he will always protect us physically from everything, though certainly God can, and he does watch over us all the time. This is the kindness of God's common grace. As our Creator who is both sovereign and good, God chooses to protect his creation. Why aren't more people harmed by evil each day? Why hasn't our world disintegrated by now at evil's hands? Because God has been merciful, keeping much evil from happening by his restraining, supernatural power.

Often, when we think about evil, we see ourselves and other people as victims—and in one sense, that's true. My friend and I were victimized by a gunman that night in my car. Concertgoers in Las Vegas became victims of an insane shooter. Christians persecuted for their faith are victims of hateful violence. But our perspective shifts when we realize that evil isn't just "out there" but is within each person's heart. Every human being inherited Adam's sin and the inclination to turn from fearing God to rebelling against him. *We are not solely victims of evil; rather, that same evil naturally resides in us.* By nature, we are God's enemies.

So if evil dwells within all humankind, why aren't things worse than they are? Jerry Bridges writes: "God can restrain not only people's actions, but even their most deeply rooted desires. No part of the human heart is impervious to God's sovereign but mysterious control."[1] Somehow God, in his infinite wisdom and power, works (and has worked) in the minds and hearts of men to keep them from doing what they're capable of doing. This goes for you and me—*all of us* are capable of terrible atrocities because sin has corrupted all of creation through the fall.

You may think, *I'd never do what those people are doing.* But how do you know this? You don't, because God has mercifully restrained evil within you. He has ordered and ordained your circumstances to keep such atrocities from coming to pass. Things aren't as bad as they could be because God restrains evil in *every creature* on a daily basis, and this is his mercy and protection.

God protects his people from Satan.

Scripture testifies to another way God protects us: from our greatest foe, Satan, who "prowls around like a roaring lion, seeking someone to devour" (1 Peter 5:8); who delights to tempt us into sin, which leads to death (James 1:14–15); and whose goal it is to destroy our faith by accusing us with lies and assailing us with doubts (John 8:44). God's promise to protect us from him is sure: "I give them eternal life, and they will never perish, and no one will snatch them out of my hand" (John 10:28).

But what about the enemy's evil schemes, especially in the lives of God's people? Consider Job, who loved and followed the Lord but was assailed by the devil. John Piper writes of this account,

> God is sovereign over Satan. The devil does not have a free hand in this world. He is on a leash, so that he can do no more than God permits. In effect, he must get permission—as in the case of . . . Job: "The Lord said to Satan, 'Behold, Job is in your hand; only spare his life'" (Job 2:6).[2]

This may seem like the opposite of protection, as we wonder why God would allow Satan any freedom, but *we must remember who is holding the leash. He is sovereign and good.* This means we can trust God's character and purposes as he gives Satan temporary permissions that somehow, in a grand mystery, fulfill his will for his people and ultimately for his glory.

Lest we think that God and Satan wield the same authority in some kind of cosmic battle for power, we must remember that the cross accomplished the defeat of the forces of evil: "[God] disarmed the rulers and authorities and put them to open shame, by triumphing over them in [Christ]" (Colossians 2:15). Though he once reigned over us, blinding us to sin and leading us to our death, now our enemy has been disarmed and dethroned, as the King of kings has ascended to the Father's right hand and taken his rightful place on the throne of our hearts. Those who've trusted in Jesus are "being guarded" from the devil's power "by God's power . . . through faith for a salvation ready to be revealed in the last time" (1 Peter 1:5).

Satan may entice and accuse God's people, but we have the whole armor of God by which to stand against his schemes (Ephesians 6), and even as he attempts to steal from, kill, and destroy us, we know we've been given life in abundance through Jesus Christ (John 10:10), who "protects [us], and the evil one does not touch [us]" (1 John 5:18).

God protects his people from his wrath.

If Satan had his way, he'd delight to see us all receive the wages of our sin, which is eternal death under the wrath of God (Romans 6:23). Remember that God's wrath is his righteous and just anger toward the sin that offends his holiness. In chapter 1, we saw how the evil of sin distorted our fear of God and brought all humankind under his wrath, which is "revealed from heaven against all ungodliness and unrighteousness of men" (Romans 1:18). God's wrath is a "necessary reaction to objective moral evil," says Packer[3]—and this "moral evil" dwells within us, turning our awe of God into terror before him.

Truly, to remain under God's wrath now and forever should be one of the things a person fears most.

But as believers in Christ, we should simultaneously stand in awe of God's great and loving mercy to protect us from it, which he has done in two primary ways. First, he has protected us from *his present wrath* that's revealed in the seared consciences and hardened hearts of unrepentant sinners:

> For although they knew God, they did not honor him as God or give thanks to him, but they became futile in their thinking, and their foolish hearts were darkened. . . . Therefore God gave them up in the lusts of their hearts. . . . And since they did not see fit to acknowledge God, God gave them up to a debased mind to do what ought not to be done.
>
> Romans 1:21, 24, 28

We see evidence all around us of sin's evil power and its destructive desires within the hearts of men, and Scripture says that God has given (and will give) them what they desire. But God has protected believers from this present form of his wrath through the gift of new hearts that instead desire and fear him. We are "being renewed in knowledge after the image of [our] creator" (Colossians 3:10) as we put off sin and put on the Lord Jesus Christ—even as we fight fear.

Second, God has protected us from *his coming wrath* that will be revealed when Jesus returns. One day soon God's Son will come on the clouds with glory, and he will take his seat on his judgment throne (more on this in chapter 9). Every one of us will appear before him to "receive what is due for what [we have] done in the body, whether good or evil" (2 Corinthians 5:10). Those who have rejected Christ's gift of salvation will be cast into the outer darkness where there will be weeping and gnashing of teeth (Matthew 22:13; Luke 13:28). But God will protect all those who have received Christ by faith.

He does so on the basis of the cross, where the wrath we deserve fell upon Jesus instead.

In his Son, God sends us a Rescuer who made the ascent to Jerusalem through evils of temptation, abandonment, torture, and crucifixion. There on the cross, Jesus became sin for us and absorbed God's wrath in our place, dying the death we deserve. He became the Victor, who ransoms us from bondage to evil by paying the debt we owe, and he fulfills God's covenant promise to give his people new desires to fear him as he removes our stony, evil hearts and replaces them with hearts of flesh (Ezekiel 36:26). Because Jesus exposed himself to many evils—and the primary evil of all, death—those who know him never need to fear evil's power again:

> The sting of death is sin, and the power of sin is the law. But thanks be to God, who gives us the victory through our Lord Jesus Christ.
>
> 1 Corinthians 15:56–57

The Lord Will Keep You . . . Forevermore

As God's promise of ultimate victory eases our fears, one more aspect of this protection will give us courage in the face of evil: *God will deal with it and give evil and the evildoer what they deserve.*

Through the justice system, we see inklings of this promise fulfilled now on earth—but justice isn't always served, nor does earthly justice fulfill what God has in store for his enemies. As the cross of Christ promises death's final defeat, so the return of Christ will secure the promise. At this moment, the martyrs in heaven groan for the fulfillment of it: "O Sovereign Lord, holy and true, how long before you will judge and avenge our blood on those who dwell on the earth?" (Revelation 6:10). Here on earth, we long to see evil dealt with once for all, avenged by Jesus, who will come with a sword in his mouth and blood on his robe to save us—to protect us—forever.

Take in this stunning picture from Revelation:

> Then I saw heaven opened, and behold, a white horse! The one sitting on it is called Faithful and True, and in righteousness he judges and makes war. His eyes are like a flame of fire, and on his head are many diadems, and he has a name written that no one knows but himself. He is clothed in a robe dipped in blood, and the name by which he is called is The Word of God. And the armies of heaven, arrayed in fine linen, white and pure, were following him on white horses. From his mouth comes a sharp sword with which to strike down the nations, and he will rule them with a rod of iron. He will tread the winepress of the fury of the wrath of God the Almighty. On his robe and on his thigh he has a name written, King of kings and Lord of lords.
>
> Revelation 19:11–16

Friend, even if your life is lost at the hands of evil, even if the danger you most fear comes to pass, evildoers may hurt your body, but they cannot touch your soul. You are ultimately protected by your victorious King Jesus, and God will avenge every evil committed against you: "The God of peace will soon crush Satan under your feet. The grace of our Lord Jesus Christ be with you" (Romans 16:20). Lift your eyes to your Keeper—bring your fears to him—and see where your help comes from.

LEARNING TO TRUST

PONDER. Memorize Psalm 121:7–8: "The Lord will keep you from all evil; he will keep your life. The Lord will keep your going out and your coming in from this time forth and forevermore."

PRESERVE. Can you think of times when you clearly saw God protect you from harmful circumstances?

PREPARE. Ephesians 6:11 (NIV) says, "Put on the full armor of God, so that you can take your stand against the devil's schemes." What would it look like for you to "put on" his armor?

PRAY. *God, my Keeper, my help comes from you, who made heaven and earth. You are my Creator and Sustainer, and I want to trust you when you say you'll protect me. Mostly, I want to trust that my greatest need for safety has been met in Jesus Christ and that he goes with me today. Help me to trust that nothing can happen to me apart from your perfect will and to know that I don't need to be afraid, since no one can touch my soul. In Jesus' name, amen.*

The Lord will keep you
from all evil;
he will keep your life.
The Lord will keep
your going out
and your coming in
from this time forth and
forevermore.

PSALM 121:7-8

seven

I WILL NEVER LEAVE YOU
(When You Fear Loneliness)

God has said, "Never will I leave you; never will I forsake you."

Hebrews 13:5 NIV

A CERTAIN HEALTH CRISIS in America has become widespread across the decades. It afflicts more of us than we realize: the young as well as the old, the well-off and the poor, men and women alike. It is not always obvious, its compounding effect weighing upon our minds and bodies and possibly "hastening millions of people to an early grave,"[1] according to authors John Cacioppo and William Patrick.

It's the loneliness epidemic.[2]

Scientists and doctors are calling it one of America's biggest unseen problems as they observe the great toll it has taken on our well-being. We may live in a culture that's more connected than ever thanks to modern technology, but we're ironically all the more lonely for it and increasingly affected by it, heart and soul.

Senator and author Ben Sasse comments on the gravity of the loneliness epidemic:

> The average American has gone from more than three to fewer than two intimate, flesh-and-blood actual friends over the last three decades.
>
> More alarmingly, the number of Americans who count no friends at all—no one in whom they confide about important matters, no one with whom they share life's joys and burdens—has soared. In the mid-2000s, one-quarter of Americans said they had no one with whom to talk about things that matter.[3]

No one. Not one person with whom to share life's joys and troubles. Loneliness is a pervasive and sad and *human* plight, and as such, the fear of being lonely surely follows us around, either haunting us because we've known its sting, or threatening us with its possibility.

Created for Relationships

Loneliness is not a welcome reality, but it certainly is a universal one. Author Lydia Brownback, in her book *Finding God in My Loneliness*, points out that every one of us is made for eternal fellowship with our Creator: "The primary reason we are lonely is that we aren't home yet. God created us for communion with him, and therefore loneliness will be fully eradicated only when we get to heaven. That's why everyone . . . experiences loneliness. No one is exempt."[4]

Remember that when sin distorted our fear of the Lord and awe of God became terror before him, Adam and Eve's inclination was to hide. Sin alienated us from perfect, unbroken fellowship with our holy God and within our relationships, and because of this, loneliness is now inevitable. But Brownback points us to our hope: "Loneliness is an indicator that something is missing, and that something is found only in Jesus Christ."[5]

Only when we are reconciled to God through our Savior and Mediator can we say we're never alone, even when we're lonely. Only through our living union with Jesus Christ can we be confident, despite our feelings and circumstances, that he's with us in the room right now. And only when we're given a new heart and the promised Holy Spirit—the very presence of Jesus dwelling within us—can we fight fears related to loneliness.

Afraid of Loneliness

My loneliest life-season was spent in bustling New York City, thirteen hours away from home—the definition of being alone in a crowd. I'd moved there to pursue my acting dream, and to see if the long-distance relationship I was in would lead to marriage. But none of it worked out: I broke up with my then-boyfriend, got zero jobs in the theater world, and worked twelve-hour days just to make ends meet. Usually, I was sad and discouraged and incredibly lonely—even though most of my time was spent riding on a crowded subway or traversing busy streets along with millions of other people.

Many of you are lonely, whether you're physically separated from loved ones as I was, or you're aching from singleness or childlessness or grief, or you're surrounded by people who either don't care about or can't enter into your pain. And you're afraid—afraid of feeling this way forever, afraid of the emotional isolation that comes from intense suffering that no one else can fully fathom, afraid of alienation from the culture or being abandoned by the people you care about most.

In this chapter, we're going to explore each of these aspects of loneliness by entering into the stories of five real people. And we'll see how God's promise in Hebrews 13:5 (NIV)—"Never will I leave you; never will I forsake you"—can be trusted in every lonely circumstance and the fears that often accompany them.

The Pain of Abandonment—Caitlin's Story

If you've ever been rejected or abandoned by people you trusted (or wanted to trust), you know the fear that such loneliness leaves in its wake. You become afraid that other relationships will end the same way, that you're not enough, and that your future will be one of loneliness. Caitlin, who's been my friend for almost a decade, has known the rejection of important people who should have been there for her:

> I have been abandoned twice. The first was when my father left us after sixteen years of abuse and neglect. The second came suddenly when the man I was going to marry simply changed his mind.
>
> I've grieved these losses because they have all the finality, confusion, and sadness of death, with the added pain of knowing that both of these men left by choice. It's the pain of being discarded, rejected, unwanted, and it carries a lot of shame.[6]

Caitlin describes being abandoned by loved ones as *loss*. She grieves—and grief doesn't disappear overnight. Processing the death of relationships not only takes time, it takes trust in Jesus, the only One who never changes or leaves:

> But because of Christ, I have hope.
>
> Jesus Christ, who is fully God but also fully a man, gave his life to make me his so that I would be loved and blameless (Ephesians 1:4). He promises to never leave me (Hebrews 13:5), and he is incapable of changing his mind.[7]

Over the years, I've been so encouraged by God's work within Caitlin: He's taught her what it looks like to trust him as her faithful, always-present Father even when human trust has been compromised.

Alone in a City Full of People—Katie's Story

Have you ever been the new person in town? There's a loneliness that comes from being planted in a new place where everyone but you seems comfortable and established. From that loneliness comes the fear that you'll never find where you fit.

This is my sister's story. Katie moved from Illinois to Arizona for a new job and soon discovered how lonely she was:

> There was a natural fear of being lonely when I moved [to Arizona], one that I had really never felt before. . . . I didn't feel known, and that took a toll on me. After about six months . . . I was put on an

anxiety medicine to help with various health things. Ultimately, that made me feel even lonelier. The medicine numbed any form of emotion, positive or negative. I soon realized that no medicine would cover up the feeling of anxiousness I had in trying to build a consistent healthy community.

The only real way to [do this] involved me putting myself out there and allowing others to let me in and care for me, while being consistent in trying new things. I joined my church's worship team in February of 2017 and . . . beginning to attend a young adults' group at church not only gave me people to be around, but people who actually loved and cared about me.[8]

God used a local church to help Katie fight her fears over her loneliness. As God provided his people for her, so God gives us his church as a manifestation of his presence. Katie has learned that her church family is a wonderful picture of the God who is always with her, and who has delighted to show her, in unexpected ways, who he is. She says,

Ultimately, God does not give us opportunities and answers when we might desire them. . . . It is freeing when God provides community for us in his timing, because in that feeling of loneliness we begin to discover a lot more about God's identity. He is consistent, all-loving, and he will never abandon us. He never abandoned me, even when I felt at my lowest of lows. He heard me, saw me, listened to me, and provided.[9]

In her loneliness, my sister learned to trust God's promise to never leave or forsake her, a promise grounded in his unchanging character and faithful presence. Similarly, our fear of loneliness is an opportunity to learn more of who God is: our steadfast anchor amid change, our comfort when we're uncomfortable, and our near friend whom we know better and treasure more when earthly companions feel far from us.

***

Standing Alone for Christ—Dan's Story

Dan leads music at our church and is executive director of a non-profit ministry whose mission is to show the compassion of Christ to refugees and their children. I asked Dan to comment on the unique loneliness of following Jesus in cultures opposed to him, and he shared the following story about one of his international trips:

> "Are you a journalist?" one of the soldiers asked.
>
> My hands were extended to the sky. I was surrounded by eight other soldiers, machine guns strapped around their shoulders. I was afraid that I would be sent to prison for a crime that I willingly committed.
>
> "No," I answered, leaving out the fact that I had recently quit my job as a journalist. But this was no time to parse details. "I am here on business. I'm interested in investing in this farm."
>
> That second part was true as well. Our ministry was interested in investing in the farm we were standing on because it was right on the border. I could see the dark country from where we were standing. Refugees who cross the border for relief are treated as criminals. It is legal to murder a refugee, with no action taken against the murderer. It is illegal to give a bowl of rice to one of these poor souls.[10]

Dan was terrified at the border that day. His wife and children were in America, waiting for him to return. Then things got worse:

> The soldiers began to search the car we came in and found my laptop, which held contact information for every refugee we had ever helped. If they found the addresses, not only would I be in trouble, but all the refugees in our network would be sent back to face torture and execution.
>
> "Open your computer and log in," said the soldier.
>
> I remember the immense sense of desperation and loneliness I felt as I gazed up at the winter sky. I hadn't the capacity for a long, eloquent prayer. So in my heart I prayed over and over, "God, help me." I had always been taught that God would be with me in my darkest moment, but now it was hard to believe it. I felt alone on an island, and like my prayers were bouncing around an echo chamber.
>
> "Show me your pictures," the soldier said to me.
>
> I didn't have any photos on my work laptop, or so I thought. I pulled up iPhoto and about 100 pictures of my children came up.
>
> That was all they wanted to see. He closed my computer, handed it to me, and told me to leave the country.[11]

Dan returned to the United States rattled and in shock:

> It took me weeks to snap out of the shock I was in. Perhaps it was the guns and soldiers, perhaps it was the fact that I had put so many people at risk that day, but I think the shock was from how alone I felt. I had to remind myself that I wasn't alone, that God was very much present as I faced danger and fear.
>
> David, a man familiar with danger and fear, said in Psalm 23 that "even though I walk in the valley of the shadow of death, I

will fear no evil for you are with me." I wish I were so brave. But that does not matter. For it was not the strength of my faith that saved me that lonely day, it was the strength of the One my feeble hands were holding onto.[12]

Few of us have a story as intense as Dan's from a hostile country, but many of us know the loneliness of identifying with Jesus in Christless cultures. Dan reminds us that the promise of our Savior's nearness is our strength, especially when we fear criticism, alienation, violence, and even death, from those opposed to him.

No Place to Call Home—Felicity's Story

I met Felicity after her family moved from the north of England to the US for her husband's job. She describes what it was like to make this transition to the States and raise two young boys in a new and faraway place:

> I was full of trepidation at the thought of moving continents and making our home in a different context, with a different culture and amongst different people. . . . I don't think I doubted that we would make friends, but I was fearful that we wouldn't find the depth of relationship we had so enjoyed and treasured in the UK. . . . Ultimately, I was fearful of being lonely—of being far from those I loved, and who loved me, and separated by a significant time difference as well as the obvious geographical distance. . . .
>
> Gradually, through getting stuck into a church family, seeking to meet up with people whenever possible, and praying for

meaningful get-to-know-you conversations, we began to feel like we had the beginnings of friendships. . . . We were reminded frequently that God was with us throughout all the change, and had provided for us in so many ways to counter that fear of loneliness.[13]

After only three months of getting settled in Illinois, Felicity and her boys found themselves back on a plane to England, after her husband was denied reentrance to the States while overseas on business. The uprootedness continued for them as they settled back in the UK:

To find ourselves suddenly not in our home and without those burgeoning relationships was an experience that had us reeling for several weeks. It was a strange thing to have said goodbye to our friends and family, setting up the expectation that we'd be out of the country, and now we were back—without a home, and without any real idea of how long we would be around. I'm thankful for the love and support of family and friends, and we have felt very loved amidst it all. But it is an isolating experience to uproot, make your home, and then uproot again. We were caught in a no-man's land.[14]

The yearning for an earthly home has revealed to Felicity and her family the surety and stability of their heavenly home and has led them to trust God in new ways during this season of loneliness. In my friend, I've seen a deep well of assurance in Jesus:

My stability doesn't come from bricks and mortar or having a visa, but from being unchangeably secure in Christ. Visa or no visa, home or no home, I remain certain that I'm hidden in him.

The promise from Hebrews [13:5] that God will never leave me or forsake me echoes throughout the truths I've been clinging to. . . . As a family, we are trusting God more than we ever have, and that is reflected in the way we pray and read His word, as we are reminded again and again that He is with us, and comforted by that reality. . . . It's been a privilege in some ways to have everything stripped back, and so to know that it really is God alone who is with us always—however many relationships and support networks we cultivate. He alone is unchanging, faithful, and will never leave us.[15]

When No One Understands—Sarah's Story

Sarah is another dear friend and coauthor of the book we wrote together, *Hope When It Hurts*. For the last twelve years, she and her family have walked roads of intense suffering, including health problems, financial crisis, and parenting a son with special needs. Sarah says this about the loneliness she lives in every day:

I remember when we began realizing that my eldest son struggled in ways that other children seemed not to. When the struggles turned into life-altering challenges, I left social events, stores, and church feeling increasingly lonely. I was on a scary journey that it seemed no one else could relate to.

. . . I found myself pulling away from those I cared about. . . . I felt utterly alone. Yes, there were those who tried to ask questions, offer their suggestions . . . but it always fell short of any real solace. No one could truly enter into the pain, heartache, and loneliness growing in my home and within my heart.[16]

Maybe you relate to Sarah, and it seems like no one can empathize with your suffering. Maybe the fear of being isolated in pain, that you'll never know the comfort of being understood, resonates with you. Maybe you're afraid of the pent-up stress and turmoil within you and are unsure of how to express what's going on in your heart.

How does God's promise to be with you in the loneliness of suffering—and any loneliness, for that matter—apply to your fears? Sarah has learned to trust 2 Corinthians 1:3: "Blessed be the God and Father of our Lord Jesus Christ, the Father of mercies and God of all comfort." We'll end with these powerful truths, which Sarah has put so beautifully:

> There is only one God of all comfort, and he does not sleep in your house or park next [to] you outside your church. He is Jesus. . . .
>
> . . . Jesus knows the pain of loneliness. He knows the loneliness of being misunderstood, the loneliness of being rejected by his own family, the loneliness of praying in agony while his closest friends drifted off to sleep nearby, and the loneliness of being abandoned by his Father. *And he did it all for you.* We may experience loneliness on many levels but because he went before us, we will never have to experience the crushing loneliness of separation from God the Father, as he did. Our loving Father sent his own Son down the loneliest road ever known to man so that we would never have to walk any road apart from him.[17]

LEARNING TO TRUST

PONDER. Memorize Hebrews 13:5 (NIV): "God has said, 'Never will I leave you; never will I forsake you.'"

PRESERVE. Revisit believers' stories of trusting God in their loneliness. Seek biblical accounts of God's presence with his people (e.g., Joseph, Genesis 37–50; Joshua, Deuteronomy 31; and Paul, 2 Corinthians 11–12.)

PREPARE. Remember how God has fulfilled his covenant-promise to you by giving you himself. John Flavel shows us how this dispels fear when we are lonely: "If you are within the bonds of the covenant, you will surely find enough there to quiet your heart—whatever the cause of your fear. If God is your covenant-God, He will be with you in all your straits, wants, and troubles. He will never leave you nor forsake you."[18]

PRAY. *Ever-present Father, you know the depths of my loneliness and my great desire for relationship, which you made me for. Thank you for giving your Son to walk the loneliest road, so I would never be alone but know your intimate presence forever. When I'm lonely and afraid of the loneliness, comfort me with your Spirit and with other believers. Deepen my trust that you will never leave me or forsake me. In Jesus' name, amen.*

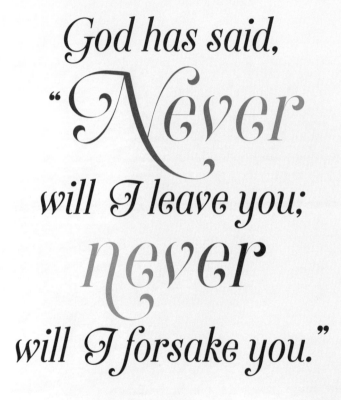

God has said, "Never will I leave you; never will I forsake you."

HEBREWS 13:5

eight

I HAVE ACCEPTED YOU

(When You Fear Failure)

And to the one who does not work but believes in him who
justifies the ungodly, his faith is counted as righteousness.

Romans 4:5

SEVERAL YEARS BACK, I worked in the children's ministry department of our church. Since I had a background in
music, my boss tasked me with composing an original song for the
kids to sing in worship services on Easter Sunday. I got to work
writing a simple melody with lyrics based on Psalm 67 and then
recorded myself singing and playing the piano so the kids could
easily follow along.

Two hundred burned CDs later, I had the parents pick up the
music the following Sunday at church. I encouraged them to play

it often over the next few weeks leading up to Easter: at home, in the car, and wherever and whenever they could.

That is, until I got urgent phone calls from some very concerned parents.

Apparently, the software I had used to burn the CDs had somehow changed my song titles into random expletives. To this day, I have no idea how this happened, and I was *mortified*. Those poor kids! I immediately emailed the parents to apologize and asked them to destroy the CDs.

It was the definition of an epic failure.

The Sting of Failure

If I asked you to remember a time when you failed, you'd probably not have to think too long or hard about it. Avoiding failure is like trying to evade death—impossible, regardless of how hard we strive against it. Failure often embarrasses and shames us, and therefore, it gets imprinted upon our memories like a scar upon impressionable flesh. Of course, some failures are more like inconspicuous marks rather than gaping wounds, but regardless, failure always *stings*.

Perhaps failure after failure has seemed to define you, and you feel stuck, unable to change, and afraid of the patterns you can't break. But what you need to know is this: God's promise of acceptance is for you.

Or maybe you're a perfectionist, and a good kind of determination can quickly devolve into an exhausting and fear-driven pursuit of the unattainable. God's promise of acceptance is equally for you.

And God's promise is also for those who've gone before us. Even the many heroes of the faith—the well-known men and women of the Bible—might more accurately be called *failures who had faith*. They too operated from distorted fears that led to sin against God and others, to missteps that couldn't be erased, and to a merciful awareness of their need for God's intervention. Here are some of their stories.

Eve: Mothering the First Murderer

"The mother of humanity was also the mother of the world's first murderer."[1] Can you fathom Eve's grief and shame when she heard that her firstborn son had killed his brother? Perhaps her damning decision in the garden flashed through her mind when she heard about Abel's brutal murder: *This is my fault. I brought this on our family.*

We who are parents relate to Eve. We taste her humiliation, fearing that the foolish choices we've made will forever impact our children, and us. It's no stretch of the imagination to enter into Adam and Eve's sin-laden failure, because we're the unfortunate descendants of it: "Therefore, just as sin came into the world through one man, and death through sin, and so death spread to all men because all sinned" (Romans 5:12).

Since all have sinned, we've not only failed our kids, our kids have failed us—which makes us rehearse anew all the ways we've failed them as parents. And the cycle continues.

Abraham: Looking Out for Number One

Next, we turn to Abraham. The same man who received God's undeserved favor struggled with a self-sufficient, fearful heart, even though God had said he would become the father of many:

> Now the Lord said to Abram, "Go from your country and your kindred and your father's house to the land that I will show you. And I will make of you a great nation, and I will bless you and make your name great, so that you will be a blessing. I will bless those who bless you, and him who dishonors you I will curse, and in you all the families of the earth shall be blessed."
>
> Genesis 12:1–3

Despite God's promise that he would beget a great nation, Abraham lied about his wife's identity twice in foreign lands, fearing the people there would kill him (Genesis 12:10–20). He also went along with the plan formulated by his wife, Sarah, trying to fulfill God's word through his female servant rather than his wife (Genesis 16).

Abraham's story speaks to those of us who feel like failures in specific contexts: at work, at home, or in relationships. We doubt God's Word and forget his presence, we cower in difficult circumstances and fear man rather than God (more on this in the next chapter), and we disappoint, even betray, those we care about. Protecting ourselves and our pride, we take matters into our own hands rather than entrusting ourselves and our circumstances to the One who is sovereign and good.

Aaron: Leading a Nation into Idolatry

God appointed Moses to represent his people in Egypt, guide them during Passover, and deliver them through the Red Sea. Yet, despite seeing God's almighty hand in overcoming their enemies and rescuing them to freedom, the people continually grumbled against their leader and ultimately their God (Exodus 16:2, 17:3). When Moses went to receive God's commandments on Mount Sinai he left Aaron in charge, but the people complained to him too:

> When the people saw that Moses delayed to come down from the mountain, the people gathered themselves together to Aaron and said to him, "Up, make us gods who shall go before us. As for this Moses, the man who brought us up out of the land of Egypt, we do not know what has become of him."
>
> Exodus 32:1

Not surprisingly, Aaron caved under the pressure. He instructed the people to give him their gold jewelry, and he melted it to fashion a golden calf. "And they said, 'These are your gods, O Israel, who brought you up out of the land of Egypt!' When Aaron saw this, he built an altar before it" (vv. 4–5). Aaron was given responsibility, but he utterly failed. He not only led poorly, he *misled* God's people into idolatry and sin. Perhaps, like Aaron, you know what it's like to be in a leadership position where you've failed to uphold your God-given responsibilities, even leading others into dangerous places.

Peter: Messing Up . . . Again

Then there's Peter. The disciple who saw Jesus transfigured on the mountain in brightness and glory, who confidently proclaimed him as "the Christ, the Son of the living God" (Matthew 16:16), also knew the sting of repeated failure: He denied his Savior three times before his crucifixion and wept bitterly for his own cowardice (Matthew 26:75).

If you've struggled to break patterns of sin, if you're burdened by repeated failures, if you've been generally discouraged by your shortcomings and sin as you walk with Christ, or if you've spent a season wandering from him, then you most likely relate to Peter. You wonder if it's possible to exhaust God's patience and if there's more you could be doing to please him.

Paul: Persecuting the Church

Perhaps the most excruciating profile of failure is that of Paul, who unashamedly persecuted Christians: "Saul was ravaging the church, and entering house after house, he dragged off men and women and committed them to prison" (Acts 8:3). But Jesus miraculously came to Paul, blinding the murderer while opening his eyes to his glory:

> Now as he went on his way, he approached Damascus, and suddenly a light from heaven shone around him. And falling to the ground, he heard a voice saying to him, "Saul, Saul, why are you persecuting me?" And he said, "Who are you, Lord?" And he said, "I am Jesus, whom you are persecuting."
>
> Acts 9:3–5

After Paul's conversion to Christ, we read about his entrance into the synagogue. Many trembled in fear before him, and the amazement of the believers over Paul's genuineness (9:21) probably also resided within the former murderer himself. *How could a person with such a wretched past be one of God's own? How could so much sin be forgiven?* Many of us wonder the same about ourselves (and others) as we look on past failures and doubt there's any hope for forgiveness.

Forgetting Our Great God

As these biblical accounts portray, there's nothing new under the sun when it comes to human failure. I recognize myself, and fears from my past and present, within each of them. My point in sharing them is twofold: First, to help you see that God's Word is always relevant, exposing the human heart and touching every part of our lives today; and second, to demonstrate that God's Word isn't about great men and women, but a great and strong God.

So much of our fear of failure, and our resistance toward anything that will make us look weak and incapable, comes from *forgetfulness.* We forget that only God is *God,* perfect in power, wisdom, and character. We forget that we are not like him, that he made us flesh-bound creatures—molded in his image, yes, but with limitations that are good for us because they keep us dependent on him. We forget how lifeless and empty and foolish are the world's messages that deceive us into thinking *we've got this* and *we're enough*—until we don't "got this" and we're clearly not enough, and so we feel even worse than when we started.

And we forget the great extent of God's mercy and grace for sinners, that he has promised to accept us through the saving work of his Son: "And to the one who does not work but believes in him who justifies the ungodly, his faith is counted as righteousness" (Romans 4:5).

What's the basis for such a magnificent promise as this? How can this be? The grounds of our acceptance are not our earning it; nor does God simply sweep our sins under the rug, as so many like to believe. The basis of God accepting us, as Romans 4:5 states, is that "[he will *justify*] the ungodly" who believe in him by faith in Jesus Christ.

But what does "justify" mean?

An Astonishing Reality

In Romans 5:6 we get our first clue toward a definition: "While we were still weak, at the right time Christ died for the ungodly." Jesus, the God-man and the epitome of godliness, did what ungodly and forgetful sinners could never do: He feared God with perfection—he worshiped and revered him, and him alone—all the way to the cross, where he became the acceptable sacrifice for our sin. He took our place upon the tree, because we, in our ungodliness, could never earn God's acceptance and because God, in his righteousness, could never justly sweep our sins under the rug.

Think about all the ways Jesus succeeded where God's people failed:

- Eve gave in to the serpent's lies in the garden, casting humankind into sin. Jesus withstood Satan's lies in the wilderness (Matthew 4) and was without sin, to redeem humankind from sin.
- Abraham sought self-protection, ease, and his own will. Jesus gave up his heavenly rights and comforts and sought to do his Father's will (John 6:38).

- Aaron feared men, giving in to the Israelites' demands. Jesus feared his Father and was never swayed by the demands of the crowds (John 6:15).
- Peter denied Jesus when he was questioned by a slave girl. Jesus never denied his Father, even under questions, threats, and abuse from Roman high officials.
- Paul shed the blood of Christians. Jesus shed his blood for Paul.

On the cross, Jesus became sin—he became our unacceptability before God—so we might become his righteousness and be accepted by God.

This is what many have called the Great Exchange. In God's compassion and love toward ungodly and forgetful sinners, he gave his only Son, so that "to the one who does not work but believes in him who justifies the ungodly, his faith is counted as righteousness" (Romans 4:5). The grounds for God's acceptance of his people, then, involves this astounding exchange, called *imputation*: our sins upon Jesus, his sinlessness upon us.

Through imputation, God legally declares that we have righteous standing before him. Justification, then, means that an ungodly sinner has received Christ's sinless record and has been declared righteous in God's sight. It means the Great Exchange has been accomplished by Jesus on the sinner's behalf. It means, in John Calvin's words, that we are "both reckoned righteous in God's judgment and [have] been accepted on account of his righteousness."[2]

Justification means, in these astonishing words, that it's *just as if we had never sinned.*

Freedom from Failure's Shame

We shouldn't miss the fact that Paul, the former murderer, penned the letter to the Romans, where this wonderful promise of acceptance lives. Through the inspiration of the Holy Spirit, Paul composed a book overflowing with the good news about Jesus Christ,[3] proclaiming how unacceptable sinners can be accepted by God through faith in him. Paul knew the depths of his sin, but also that God's justifying grace runs deeper. He knew the history of his failures, and the failures of every human, but also that Jesus came for failures, for those who know they don't have what it takes. Jared Wilson calls this "good news for losers," writing, "What Jesus has done is good news *only* for losers. If you're not a loser, in fact, you can't have Jesus."[4]

Do you know that you're a loser? Do you know that striving against sin and failure in your own strength is a useless and exhausting pursuit? Do you realize that justification isn't about being a good person but confessing that you aren't one? Men and women who throw up their hands in defeat, who know their need of Christ and lay hold of him by faith, *God justifies*. He declares you righteous and accepts you into his favor and his family, not because you are good or worthy or awesome, but because *he is*, and he delights to share his goodness—his righteousness—with you.

Could you have any more confident assurance and freedom from the shame of your failures than this? "For the Scripture says, 'Everyone who believes in [Jesus] will not be put to shame'" (Romans 10:11).

Fight with These Three Truths

Yet our struggle with forgetfulness won't cease until we see the One in whom we have believed by faith. Because our flesh is weak, the world is alluring, and our enemy accuses us, we need to fight every day for the truth of the gospel message to fill our minds and penetrate our hearts. So, when you're struggling with the fear of failure—when you've forgotten who Jesus is and what he has accomplished for his people—tell yourself these three truths, taken from Paul's words in Romans 5:

God's promise is trustworthy and true.

"Therefore, since we have been justified by faith, we have peace with God through our Lord Jesus Christ" (v. 1). If you have laid hold of Jesus Christ by faith, have seen your need for him, and have believed that his work on your behalf is finished, then you can trust without a doubt that God has accepted you into his family. Declare to your own heart what God has declared in the heavenly places: *I am justified in Jesus Christ. Yes, I have sinned and failed, but Jesus came for this, to bear my sin and remove my guilt. I am at peace with God. He has accepted me.*

God's glory is the goal.

"Through [Christ] we have also obtained access by faith into this grace in which we stand, and we rejoice in hope of the glory of God" (v. 2). The end of all things and the aim for which we live is the glory of God. Think of the glory he receives—from you, from those around you, and from the unseen places—when incapable, forgetful, ungodly sinners become his through his patient kindness, his wise salvation plan, and Christ's perfect sacrifice. This means that you can rejoice and persevere even when you fail, since your hope isn't in yourself but in God who gets glory as you learn to trust and fear him.

God's Spirit is at work.

"Not only that, but we rejoice in our sufferings, knowing that suffering produces endurance, and endurance produces character, and character produces hope, and hope does not put us to shame, because God's love has been poured into our hearts through the Holy Spirit who has been given to us" (vv. 3–5). Not only did God complete a good work in you when he saved you, declaring you righteous in Christ (*justification*), he will complete a good work in you as his Spirit changes you and grows you up into Christ (*sanctification*). Because Jesus is sovereign and good, he will use your failures, even suffering, to accomplish his transforming work in you, which is ultimately for the advancement of his purposes so that many more people will be pointed to him. And you can be sure that if he starts a good work, he will finish it (*glorification*).

My friends, you and I are not unlike the saints of biblical history: We too are failures who have faith in a great Savior who has taken upon himself the sting of our scars and wounds, and whose righteousness has been permanently imprinted upon us in their place. In him, we are fully and completely accepted by our God. Yes, we will sin and we will fail, but when we do we will not forget or despair; we will trust God by telling ourselves the truth and "[believing] in him who justifies the ungodly."

LEARNING TO TRUST

PONDER. Memorize Romans 4:5: "And to the one who does not work but believes in him who justifies the ungodly, his faith is counted as righteousness."

PRESERVE. Think of a time when you failed. How did you see God at work, even through your sins and mistakes? What did you learn about his character and your need?

PREPARE. Which of the three truths taken from Romans 5 do you need to tell yourself right now?

PRAY. *Gracious and strong God, when I'm afraid of failure, help me remember that you've accepted me in Christ, and help me believe this. Pour your love into my heart through the Holy Spirit. Thank you that Jesus came for sinners who could never work our way to you, completing all that was necessary for our salvation. Thank you for receiving me into your favor and crediting your Son's righteousness to me. Use my life for your glory, failures and all, that many people will be pointed to the sufficiency and perfection of your Son. In Jesus' name, amen.*

And to the one who does not work but believes in him who justifies the ungodly, his faith is counted as righteousness.

ROMANS 4:5

nine

I WILL JUDGE YOU
(When You Fear Man)

For we must all appear before the judgment seat of Christ, so that each one may receive what is due for what he has done in the body, whether good or evil.

2 Corinthians 5:10

G REG IS A hard worker who wants to honor the Lord. His boss, however, isn't easy to please and is often critical of him, even when his job is done with excellence. Greg knows that the best way to handle his boss is to keep working with integrity and to treat him with honor and respect, even when he feels degraded. But the temptation to prove his worth and outdo his fellow employees entices him. He figures if he could just close the high-stakes deal everyone's been vying for, then his boss might respect him.

The problem is that even when Greg succeeds it's never enough, for his boss or for himself.

Morgan goes to the gym three times a week. She has struck up friendships with some women she sees in the locker room and has enjoyed getting to know them. She wonders if she'll ever get the chance to talk with them about Jesus—she doesn't get a sense they're Christians, or that they even go to church. But when she is asked one morning why she seems so happy all the time, she clams up and words fail her. She brushes off their question and resorts to humor, saying, "Oh, am I? Believe me, you don't see me when the alarm clock goes off. . . ." Later, she can't shake the nagging feeling that she blew it.

Michael leads a double life. On Sundays and Wednesdays, he is a good youth-group kid, plays guitar in the worship band, and enjoys hanging out with his church friends. But when he's not at church or around people of good influence, Michael caves to peer pressure and makes one poor decision after another. Now the dishonesty is tearing him apart, and he knows he must decide whom to follow. Jesus, or his friends?

Sue can't remember the last time she took a breath. For the last decade, she has cared for her three active kids and worked part-time from home, and she knows she's suffering the consequences of an overloaded schedule. But she has the hardest time saying no to her children, her clients, her church, her friends. She wants to believe she's doing the right thing in serving people—but she can't remember the last time she read her Bible or prayed. She can't recall when she last felt any love for the Lord or joy in him. Sue convinces herself that it's just a season, but her emptiness and exhaustion eat away at her.

Putting People in God's Place

Do you recognize these people? Maybe you see bits of Greg, Morgan, Michael, or Sue in yourself or in people you know. All of them are struggling with the fear of man, a powerful compulsion to put others in the place of God and seek human approval above his. Counselor and author Ed Welch defines the fear of man this way: "[Fear of man] includes being afraid of someone, but it extends to holding someone in awe, being controlled or mastered by people, worshipping other people, putting your trust in people, or needing people. . . . We replace God with people."[1]

What have we seen of our great God so far? We know that he's infinitely worthy to be feared, that he delights to save those who can't save themselves, that he's good and sovereign, and that he's our faithful provider, protector, and justifier. Humans are indeed made in God's image, but because we *aren't* God, we'll never be who only God can be. Yet, when we expect people to be who only God can be and put them in his place, we make them into idols. We worship the creation instead of the Creator and, as a result, we crush finite human beings beneath a weight they were never meant to bear—and we also get crushed as a result.

Or in biblical imagery, we get trapped in a snare.

Four Destructive Snares of the Fear of Man

Proverbs 29:25 says, "The fear of man lays a snare, but whoever trusts in the Lord is safe." Let's look now at how the fear of man tempts us into four distinct traps.

Snare #1: Pride

Greg's story describes the snare of pride. The temptation to idolize people's praise and approval can lead to selfish ambition, coveting, comparison, criticism, and discontentment—all of which are ultimately about *self*. If you crave attention, if your mood depends on what people say or think, if you're constantly comparing your life to other people's, if you're a workaholic, or if your goal is to lord your influence over others, you'll want to watch for the destructive snare of pride.

Snare #2: Cowardice

Many of us struggle with fear in evangelism, so we relate to Morgan's story. The Holy Spirit can help us be patient and gracious toward those who are far from Jesus. But the fear of man that's tempted by comfort, ease, and affirmation can lead to the snare of cowardice, even denying Christ. If you struggle with telling people you went to church over the weekend, if you routinely neglect talking about Jesus with others, or if you are silenced for fear of not having the right words, you'll want to watch for the snare of cowardice.

Snare #3: Disobedience

The fear of man can lead us to do things we never thought we'd do. Whether it's in the teenage boy who is pressured by his friends, as Michael was, or adults who compromise their beliefs to blend in with the crowd, the temptation to satisfy people rather than obey God can be strong. If you dislike feeling out of place in the world, if you're tempted to sin because you know God will forgive you later, or if you notice that your friends are discouraging your pursuit of Christ, you'll want to watch for the snare of disobedience.

Snare #4: Self-Sufficiency

Sue's story is the temptation every people pleaser faces. Helping, caring for, and serving others is certainly a good thing. But only God is the Savior—and how often do we try to be pseudosaviors, saying yes to everyone and everything? Similarly, only God is Lord, ruling over us with his good and kind commands, but we often let others function as little lords, telling us what to think and do. If serving God (and others) has replaced love for God, if you're constantly worried about losing people's respect or affection, or if you're regularly exhausted, you'll want to watch for the snare of self-sufficiency.

Escaping the Snares

The relieving news is that God offers his people a way out of these temptations, an escape from the destructive snares of the fear of man. 1 Corinthians 10:13 says, "No temptation has overtaken you that is not common to man"—and the fear of man is so common!—"God is faithful, and he will not let you be tempted beyond your ability, but with the temptation he will also provide the way of escape, that you may be able to endure it."

What is the way of escape that God provides for us when we're afraid of people and tempted to put them in his place? The second part of Proverbs 29:25 gives us our answer: "Whoever trusts in the Lord is safe." Safety here implies that God is our refuge, our place of hiding and security. To fight our fear of man, we must flee to the One who is to be feared—specifically into the safety of his perfect and right judgment.

God promises us in his Word that final judgment is coming: "For we must all appear before the judgment seat of Christ, so that each one may receive what is due for what he has done in the body, whether good or evil" (2 Corinthians 5:10). *We need to remember that God is our ultimate judge, not man, and that someday we will stand before his judgment seat to account for our lives.*

Scripture testifies to this promised reality in multiple places:

When the Son of Man comes in his glory, and all the angels with him, then he will sit on his glorious throne. Before him will be gathered all the nations, and he will separate people one from another as a shepherd separates the sheep from the goats.

Matthew 25:31–32

Now if anyone builds on the foundation with gold, silver, precious stones, wood, hay, straw—each one's work will become manifest, for the Day will disclose it, because it will be revealed by fire, and the fire will test what sort of work each one has done.

1 Corinthians 3:12–13

And I saw the dead, great and small, standing before the throne, and books were opened. Then another book was opened, which is the book of life. And the dead were judged by what was written in the books, according to what they had done.

Revelation 20:12

A Starkly Different Judgment

We don't know exactly what the judgment will be like, as Scripture paints only a partial picture. But we do know that God's character—including his sovereignty and his goodness—will be displayed as he judges humankind. In light of who God is, his judgment stands apart from man's in two major ways:

God's judgment is perfect, but human judgment is limited. "For the Lord sees not as man sees: man looks on the outward appearance, but the Lord looks on the heart" (1 Samuel 16:7). We're so often concerned about what people think of us when we should be concerned about what Jesus *knows* of us. God's perfect judgment means nothing is hidden from his sight. He is all-powerful, all-knowing, in control, and infinitely wise. But man's sight is limited, and so are his assessments. J. I. Packer writes, "When the Bible pictures God judging, it emphasizes his omniscience and wisdom as the searcher of hearts and the finder of facts. Nothing can escape him; we may fool men, but we cannot fool God. He knows us, and judges us, as we really are."[2]

Much of our fear of man is wrapped up in appearances, as we worry about how we come across to people and what they think of us. But before the Lord Jesus our hearts are laid bare, and we're seen for who we really are. Even in our sinful messiness, God is gracious, dealing with us in kindness and love, and not as we deserve. God knows our whole story and loves and accepts us in his Son even when man doesn't, and that fact comforts us.

God's judgment is right, but human judgment is fallible. "Shall not the Judge of all the earth do what is just?" (Genesis 18:25). Because God is holy, righteous, and always good, his judgment follows suit. He cannot err in his determinations. Consider how human judges, in a courtroom setting and with the added assistance of a jury, rule incorrectly and unjustly at times. But God, the judge of all, never gets the verdict wrong. He sees all, and in seeing all, he assesses rightly, according to his moral perfection. Since there is no spot or blemish in him, he rules with trustworthy justice. Packer writes, "The Bible leaves us in no doubt that God loves righteousness and hates iniquity, and that the ideal of a judge wholly identified with what is good and right is perfectly fulfilled in him."[3] And R.C. Sproul agrees: "There is no such thing as evil justice in God."[4]

Human judgment is fallible, but God's is always right. When people get a wrong first impression of us, or when their opinions sway their objectivity, or when justice isn't served because of human sin or error, we can cling to our just Judge and entrust ourselves to him.

Four Ways of Escape

We've seen how fearing the judgment of man compels us to please man, which lays a snare for sin—specifically the sins of pride, cowardice, disobedience, and self-sufficiency. But as we learn to fear the judgment of God, we'll be increasingly compelled to please him rather than men, and he will provide ways of escape for us.

Escape #1: The way of love

When we put people in the place of God and idolize their praise and approval, we become ensnared in pride. But as we look to Jesus, our Judge, in all his greatness and splendor and beauty, we grasp how lowly we are in comparison, and yet how loved we are by him. Our blood-bought acceptance into God's family reminds us that nothing can separate us from his love, even the disapproval of people. The vast and unchanging love of God, as proven in his Son, frees and empowers us to *love and serve people for his glory*, rather than idolize and use them for our own.

Escape #2: The way of boldness

When we put people in the place of God and fear their opposition to the good news, we become ensnared in cowardice. We avoid telling others about Jesus because we don't want to be rejected by them, or in the worst case, persecuted. But *God will never reject us*, because Jesus was rejected in our place as God's wrath was cast upon him at the cross. The thing we should most fear is God's opposition, but since God is on our side, what can man do to us (Psalm 118:6)? Men may judge us as bigots, but we rest in God's promise of acceptance and choose to love our neighbors by caring for their souls. Our eternal safety in Christ, the Judge of all, emboldens us to share the good news with those who are not yet safe in him.

Escape #3: The way of obedience

When we put people in the place of God and cave to peer pressure, we become ensnared in disobedience. But the way of escape is in obedience to God rather than men (Acts 5:29). God's Word has the final say over us, and we will be held to this standard when we appear before his throne: "For the word of God is living and active, sharper than any two-edged sword, piercing to the division of soul and of spirit, of joints and of marrow, and discerning the thoughts and intentions of the heart. And no creature is hidden from his sight, but all are naked and exposed to the eyes of him to whom we must give account" (Hebrews 4:12–13). Knowing that Jesus will judge us by his Word, we're spurred on to fear and follow him. We're willing to lose friends, even "father and mother and wife and children and brothers and sisters . . . and even [our] own life" (Luke 14:26), if it means we gain Christ for eternity.

Escape #4: The way of dependence

When we put people in the place of God and submit ourselves to their every whim and will, we become ensnared in self-sufficiency. We people-please ourselves into exhaustion and *do, do, do* for Jesus rather than resting in his work, which is *done*. We need to remember that our God-given limitations exist for a purpose: to teach us dependence upon his will and Word. Jesus gives us a sober warning about what matters most in the coming judgment when he says,

> Not everyone who says to me, "Lord, Lord," will enter the kingdom of heaven, *but the one who does the will of my Father who is in heaven.* On that day many will say to me, "Lord, Lord, did we not prophesy in your name, and cast out demons in your name, and do many mighty works in your name?" And then will I declare to them, "I never knew you; depart from me, you workers of lawlessness."
>
> Matthew 7:21–23, emphasis added

Small Steps of Faith

When it comes to love, courage, obedience, and dependence, small steps of faith can make a huge difference. Practice these, and little by little you'll find that God will strengthen you to fear him rather than men:

- Seek to actively promote others and take genuine interest in them.
- Prepare a one-minute testimony of how Jesus has saved you, and pray for opportunities to share it in everyday situations.
- Read God's Word regularly, and let him search your heart for disobedience.
- Prayerfully say no to people, even when it's hard.

An Encouraging Promise

At this point you may be wondering how the reality of God's judgment is a fear-fighting promise. But if you're worried there is a possibility of any believer losing their salvation, don't be! Remember that God gave Jesus as the sacrifice our sin requires and the mediator we most need; that in Christ, we've been counted righteous before God and are accepted by him into his family; and that there is now no condemnation for those who have laid hold of Jesus by faith. In Christ, our terror before God has become awe toward him; our rebellion against him, reverence; and our idolatrous hearts, new hearts of worship and love.

It is awe and reverence and love for Jesus that compel us to please him above man. God promises that when his people—beloved, forgiven, justified, adopted—stand before his judgment seat *we will be saved*. There is no doubt. The blood of Jesus will cover us and testify that we belong to him, forever. Still, before the judgment seat all our deeds will be exposed, and we will give an account to God for how we have feared him. This account doesn't determine our rescue, which is sure, but our rewards, which will vary according to each one's work for Christ (see 1 Corinthians 3:12–13), and this work includes how we have loved and served others, boldly invited our neighbors to Jesus, obeyed God's Word rather than men, and depended on Christ in everything.

Safe in Him

Our faith is in Christ, and our souls are preserved in him, our eternal safety and refuge. He's the perfectly right, just Judge before whom we will stand and give account—and he's our Savior, our way of escape from the snares of sin and death that once enslaved us (Psalm 18:5; Romans 6:6–7). When God's promise of judgment is fulfilled on the Last Day, those who have trusted in Jesus Christ for eternal safety will hear his "well done" and receive their reward.

Can any mere man's praise compare to that?

LEARNING TO TRUST

PONDER. Memorize 2 Corinthians 5:10: "For we must all appear before the judgment seat of Christ, so that each one may receive what is due for what he has done in the body, whether good or evil."

PRESERVE. When have you fallen into the snares of the fear of man (pride, cowardice, disobedience, self-sufficiency)? In hindsight, are you able to see how this happened? And how does identifying these snares equip you for future temptations?

PREPARE. Practice the small steps of faith outlined in this chapter: Actively promoting others, preparing and sharing your testimony, regularly reading God's Word, and prayerfully saying no to people.

PRAY. *Judge of all, you are perfect in all your ways, and that includes your judgment. Grow me in humility, courage, obedience, and dependence, and show me the way of escape when I'm tempted to be prideful, cower before men, disobey you, or rely on myself. Thank you, God, for sending your Son to free me from bondage to sin and death, and strengthen me by your Spirit to care most about your judgment. In Jesus' name, amen.*

For we must all appear before the judgment seat of Christ, so that each one may receive what is due for what he has done in the body, whether good or evil.

2 CORINTHIANS 5:10

ten

I AM ALIVE
(When You Fear Death)

*Jesus said to her, "I am the resurrection and the life. Whoever
believes in me, though he die, yet shall he live, and everyone
who lives and believes in me shall never die. Do you believe
this?"*

John 11:25–26

O F ALL THE fearful circumstances mentioned in this book,
only one is guaranteed to come to us all.

Until Jesus returns, death will arrive at the doorstep of every
man and woman, regardless of their status, geographic location, or
world view. The rich will die, along with those who spent their days
in poverty. The celebrity will die, as will the person who dwelled in
relative obscurity. The good man and the evil one will both reach

the end of their earthly existence, as well as citizens and presidents, subjects and kings alike.

Death is humanity's only guarantee. In King Solomon's words,

> It is the same for all, since the same event happens to the righteous and the wicked, to the good and the evil, to the clean and the unclean, to him who sacrifices and him who does not sacrifice. As the good one is, so is the sinner, and he who swears is as he who shuns an oath. This is an evil in all that is done under the sun, that the same event happens to all.
>
> Ecclesiastes 9:2–3

Notice how Solomon describes death as *evil*. This universal "event" is not what God intended for his creation but is a terrible outcome of the fall. "Death," says Colin Smith, "is the separating of the soul from the body, which is why death is such a fearful enemy. It is the undoing of our nature, the tearing apart of what God has joined together."[1]

When sin entered creation and distorted our fears, physical and spiritual ruin came to all men through Adam and Eve: "Therefore, just as sin came into the world through one man, and death through sin, and so death spread to all men because all sinned" (Romans 5:12). Sin corrupted the creation, darkening our hearts to the knowledge and love of God (Romans 1:21) and breaking down our temporal bodies (2 Corinthians 5:1).

Despite death's presence and gravity, many people are ambivalent toward it, saying they'll think about eternal matters when they're older. Some try to ignore it and spend their energies on evasion tactics such as antiaging products and the newest and greatest technology. Others belittle death's sting using bucket lists and morbid humor. Still others of us may be confident about what's on the other side—but if we're honest, death itself makes us uncomfortable.

Four Reasons We Fear Death

But why? What exactly is it that we're afraid of?

From my conversations about this with a number of people, it seems that our fear of death stems less from the *outcome* of it and more from its *unknowns* (although death's outcome is one reason we fear it, which we'll look at shortly). Yes, death may be a guarantee, but in many ways it's a mystery to us, and what we can't fully fathom we often fear. Specifically, there are four common reasons we're afraid of death.

The timing of our death

First, we fear death because we don't know when it will come. Death is a guarantee for every creature—"The very moment we begin to live we commence to die,"[2] says Charles Spurgeon—but its timing is mysterious. We don't know if we'll live to be ninety years old or if we'll die today. Sometimes the unknown moment of its arrival causes us to function in a state of semiparalysis; we're so afraid of dying that we struggle to do anything that might endanger us. As a result, our days are robbed of delights and dictated by fear.

John Calvin has a word for us where this is concerned:

> Suppose a man falls among thieves, or wild beasts; is shipwrecked at sea by a sudden gale; is killed by a falling house or tree. Suppose

another man wandering through the desert finds help in his straits; having been tossed by the waves, reaches harbor; miraculously escapes death by a finger's breadth. Carnal reason ascribes all such happenings . . . to fortune. But anyone who has been taught by Christ's lips that all the hairs of his head are numbered [Matt. 10:30] will . . . consider that all events are governed by God's secret plan.[3]

Our heavenly Father knows the number of hairs on our head, as well as the length of our earthly existence (Psalm 139:16). Scripture says that not even a sparrow dies apart from his knowledge (Matthew 10:29), and how much more valuable are we than sparrows (v. 31)? The Governor of the entire universe governs our days, and since he sovereignly rules in his goodness, we can trust him—even when his plan is mysterious. Even when our moment of perishing is unknown to us. Until we have reached the last day that God has written for us in his book, we cannot be touched by death. Our times are in his hand (Psalm 31:15).

The details of our death

We're also afraid of death because we don't know how it will come. This is my greatest fear regarding death: not *when* it will happen, but *how*. Many of us wonder if death will arrive suddenly and unexpectedly, or slowly with much suffering. We fear what David calls "the valley of the shadow of death" (Psalm 23:4), the darkness and pain and *details* of the inevitable.

But what David writes next is a weapon of truth in our fight against this fear: "I will fear no evil, for you are with me; your rod and your staff, they comfort me." Dr. James Merritt, in his wonderful sermon "Fear Not," comments on Jesus' faithful presence as our Shepherd, who promises to walk with and guide us, whether our valley is a short path or a winding road. He points out that the whole of the Christian life, in fact, is a walk through this valley and that when death arrives, we will fight fear as we look away from the shadow of death to the Light.[4]

Jesus, our Shepherd and our Light, knows exactly how you and I will die, and he intends to walk with us the entire way through the valley. As we saw in chapter 7, he promises to never leave us alone. The Heidelberg Catechism says it well—our only comfort in life and in death is that we belong, body and soul, to him, our faithful Savior, who will not let us go.[5]

The experience of our death

Next, we fear death because we don't know what it will be like. But Jesus has walked through death itself—bodily death, through his physical agony on the cross, and spiritual death, as he perished in the darkness of our sin and absorbed God's judgment for it in our place. Colin Smith calls the sin-bearing act of Jesus "the deepest mystery in the darkness of the cross," where the Son of God experienced the pains of hell so that we never would.[6] Most harrowing was his loss of fellowship with God as he drank the cup of his Father's wrath at Calvary (Matthew 27:46; Mark 15:34).

This would be our experience of death too if Jesus had chosen a different path, an easier one, and avoided the cross. Our fears around what it will be like to enter into death would be well-founded if Christ hadn't entered into it himself. But because he did, Jesus makes death a safe place for all those who trust him.[7] He endured death's darkness and agonies, including alienation from

God—but because he did so as our spotless Lamb, God accepted his sacrifice by raising him from the dead (Acts 13:30). Through his resurrection, Jesus triumphed over death, disabling its destructive power and transforming it into a gateway to eternal life.

Think about a soldier entering a war zone to defend his country. He endures its horrors and violence to bring about freedom, and he might die as a result—but when victory comes and the enemy surrenders, that former war zone becomes a peaceful territory, a safe place for those the soldier represents.

Apart from Christ, death is a war zone where evil abounds, sin reigns, and our enemy wins; but with Christ, death is overcome by life, evil is vanquished, sin is crucified, and the enemy is decisively defeated. When we hide ourselves in Jesus by faith, he carries us through death into the safety of everlasting life, and all the destruction that fell upon him passes over us, for our eternal freedom.

But is this safety immediate? Or is there a place where we must wait after we die until a future time? In 2 Corinthians 5:6–8, Paul insists that death leads believers *immediately* into the presence of Jesus: "We know that while we are at home in the body we are away from the Lord, for we walk by faith, not by sight. Yes, we are of good courage, and we would rather be away from the body and at home with the Lord." When our souls depart from our bodies, they go to be with Christ. No waiting, no working, no wondering—but the sure and immediate gift of Jesus.[8]

The outcome of our death

But what if you *are* wondering, and you aren't sure about what's waiting for you after you die? *Many of us fear death because we don't know what will be on the other side for us.* This is a legitimate fear that we should heed. This is God's grace. Because he created us to fear him and walk in relationship with him—because we were made for eternity—it's his *kindness* that we would be scared of a death that threatens to forever separate us from the knowledge of his love.

The fear of death is a divine wake-up call.

When the judgment comes, which it will for every person as we have seen, Jesus the judge will separate believers from unbelievers, inviting the former into his kingdom and casting the latter into eternal punishment (Matthew 25:31–46). We should fear Jesus' damning words, "Depart from me" (v. 41), and should consider what in this life is worth having if it means we don't have Christ after our death.

So the question is, Are you hidden in Jesus? Do you believe that he endured hell for your sake? Have you trusted him to bring you safely through death into his presence?

From Death to Life

In John 11, when Jesus finally arrives at Lazarus's tomb, his beloved friend has been dead four days, long enough that his sister, Martha, warns Jesus of the stench from his decaying body (v. 39). Yet Jesus *knew* Lazarus's valley of the shadow of death: He knew the moment his friend would die, he knew that sickness was the culprit that would take him, and he knew that "this illness does not lead to death. It is for the glory of God, so that the Son of God may be glorified through it" (v. 4).

Then Jesus makes a promise to Martha, which is also for those who have placed their trust in him: "I am the resurrection and the life. Whoever believes in me, though he die, yet shall he live, and everyone who lives and believes in me shall never die. Do you believe this?" (vv. 25–26). Jesus is saying, "Hide yourself in me, and I will bring you safely through death's darkness. I will unite you to myself, giving you new spiritual life right now, and I will carry you into eternal life when physical death comes."

When Jesus appears at the tomb, he commands that the stone be removed. He tells his dead friend to "come out" (v. 43). He tells the onlookers to "unbind him, and let him go" (v. 44). Jesus speaks, and death surrenders. He commands, and death capitulates. He demonstrates who he is, as the incarnate glory of God, and death's darkness flees.

This tomb scene is reminiscent of another—except on the third day after God incarnate dies, *he raises himself from the dead.* And if death could not hold the One who exposed himself to all its dimensions and horrors on the cross, then it officially and decisively loses its power over those who are hidden in him.

When you're in the grip of Jesus, death has no grip on you.

When we give ourselves to Christ, who is the resurrection and the life, the only Savior our sin requires and the Mediator we most need, we die to our former earthly selves: "I have been crucified with Christ. It is no longer I who live, but Christ who lives in me. And the life I now live in the flesh I live by faith in the Son of God, who loved me and gave himself for me" (Galatians 2:20). Commenting on this reality, Ed Welch says, "In light of the cataclysm that has already taken place at the cross, death has been robbed of some of its drama. . . . We have already died with Christ. . . . You can't die twice. If you have died with Christ, the second death has no power over you."[9]

Do you believe this?

Assurance of Life

My beautiful aunt Barbara believed it, heart and soul. Our family recently said, "Good-bye for now" to this precious woman of the Lord, who endured a long and hard battle with ovarian cancer and eventually entered the arms of her Savior. How she trusted him during her sickness and final days has both inspired and challenged me where the fear of death is concerned. When my time comes, I pray that I will trust Christ and hide myself in him as Barb did. Her lips were full of thanksgiving for her full and wonderful life as she continued to pour into those whom she would leave behind, and it was her joy to be rid of her earthly struggle and see face-to-face him in whom she had believed.

Some of you reading this are thinking, *I wish I had that confidence. At one point, I put my trust in Jesus. But my faith is so weak that I'm not sure about where I stand with him now, and I'm afraid of where I'll stand after I die.* If this is you, then your concern is most likely evidence of true and living faith, for the life of faith is sensitive to anything that would separate it from Jesus. What you need to trust right now isn't the strength of your faith but its *Object*: Jesus, the resurrection and the life, whose cross-work is finished and credited to you, who will never leave or forsake you, and whose promise of eternity is sure.

If you're afraid of death's outcome, follow my aunt Barb's example and preach to your heart about whom you have believed. Jesus has prepared a place for you, and he won't let you go:

> In my Father's house are many rooms. If it were not so, would I have told you that I go to prepare a place for you? And if I go and prepare a place for you, I will come again and will take you to

myself, that where I am you may be also. And you know the way to where I am going.

John 14:2–4

When death arrives, true and everlasting life will follow. Your King will say to you, "Come, you who are blessed by my Father, inherit the kingdom prepared for you from the foundation of the world" (Matthew 25:34). Be assured, friend, and do not fear. You will meet your Savior.

More Alive Than Ever

United to Christ, our life, we push back the fear of death. No, we do not belittle it, for death is a serious and horrible evil that should outrage us, as it did Jesus (John 11:33, 35, 38).[10] But we do not let it wither our confidence in him or steal our joy—we fight. We proclaim the gospel of death's defeat to ourselves and to those still under its curse: "That Christ died for our sins in accordance with the Scriptures, that he was buried, that he was raised on the third day in accordance with the Scriptures" (1 Corinthians 15:3–4). And we keep before our gaze the promise of death's *death*:

> For as in Adam all die, so also in Christ shall all be made alive. . . . Then comes the end, when he delivers the kingdom to God the Father after destroying every rule and every authority and power. For he must reign until he has put all his enemies under his feet. *The last enemy to be destroyed is death.*
>
> 1 Corinthians 15:22, 24–26, emphasis added

Until that day, we trust Jesus to walk with us through the valley of death's shadow, and we trust him to deliver us through it by his Spirit "who raised Christ Jesus from the dead [and] will also give life to [our] mortal bodies through his Spirit who dwells in [us]" (Romans 8:11). And so we rejoice in hope of glory, along with all the saints who've gone before us—like my aunt Barb—who now fear the Lord in his beautiful presence. One of those saints is D. L. Moody, whose proclamation of life in the Spirit we too can wield against fear:

> Some day you will read in the papers that D. L. Moody, of East Northfield, is dead. Don't you believe a word of it! At that moment I shall be more alive than I am now, I shall have gone up higher, that is all; out of this old clay tenement into a house that is immortal—a body that death cannot touch; that sin cannot taint; a body fashioned like unto His glorious body.
>
> I was born of the flesh in 1837. I was born of the Spirit in 1856. That which is born of the flesh may die. That which is born of the Spirit will live forever.[11]

LEARNING TO TRUST

PONDER. Memorize John 11:25–26: "Jesus said to her, 'I am the resurrection and the life. Whoever believes in me, though he die, yet shall he live, and everyone who lives and believes in me shall never die. Do you believe this?'"

PRESERVE. Read biographies of saints who have faced death with courage: *Through Gates of Splendor* by Elisabeth Elliot; *Bonhoeffer* by Eric Metaxas; and *Here I Stand: A Life of Martin Luther* by Roland H. Bainton.

PREPARE. Have you believed that Jesus is the resurrection and the life? If so, are you spending your life boldly for his sake, knowing you've already died with him? Who else might you prepare to meet him?

PRAY. *Lord and King Jesus, you are the resurrection and the life! You have defeated the power of sin, which is death, and removed its sting. I believe you are the only way to eternal life, and I want to live like I believe that. Make me bold, and make me serious about death and an ambassador for you so others may live in your presence too. Help me trust you with the number of my days. In your name, amen.*

Jesus said to her,
"I am the
resurrection
and the life.
Whoever believes in me,
though he die, yet shall he live,
and everyone who lives
and believes in me shall never die.
Do you believe this?"

JOHN 11:25–26

CONCLUSION

Fight Your Fears . . . and Keep Fighting

I have fought the good fight, I have finished the race, I have kept the faith.

2 Timothy 4:7

You've come to the end of this book, and you're most likely still dealing with fear. But my hope is that God's Word has given you the power and perspective you need to fight it and has helped you put your fears in their place. My prayer is that you've grown in the fear of the Lord and what it looks like to trust his character and promises when you're afraid.

And so I leave you with this truth: *Fighting your fears is like muscle memory—the more you fight, the more and better you will fight.*

Just like a piano player rehearses her music until she memorizes the sequence of notes and the song is second nature to her, and just like a track athlete trains his muscles through repetitive workouts, so we learn to fight our fears by continually coming back to Jesus and to his Word of truth.

Not *if* we're afraid, but *when* we're afraid, we wield the sword of the Spirit, which is God's Word, remembering his character and believing his promises. Trust in God doesn't necessarily mean our fears vanish but that we know where to go with them. We fight our fears with an even greater fear. So fighting your fears will be like muscle memory: As you fight them according to the truth of God's Word, that response will become more and more natural to you when those fears return or new ones arise.

And as you keep coming back to Jesus, you *will* stay in the fight. You will finish the race. You will keep the faith. And that's the goal: to know Jesus, trust him, treasure him, glorify him—

Fear him.

THANK-YOUS

WHEN I THINK about the creation of *Fight Your Fears*, many wonderful people come to mind. I am indebted to the family members, friends, and colleagues who've helped bring this project into existence.

Thank you to my at-home editorial team—my husband, Brad; my mom, Jennie; Davis Wetherell; and Julie Gernand—who read every draft of every chapter with eyes and hearts to improve upon my words. Your kind, skillful service made this book *way* better!

Truly, I'm not sure how this project would have finished if not for all the help I received from Mom, Beth, and Carol, who cared so well for our daughter while I stole away to write. I can't thank you three enough!

Thanks also to chapter 7's contributors, who eagerly shared their stories with me: Caitlin Plascencia, Felicity Carswell, Katie Evensen, Dan Chung, and Sarah Walton. Your words have been a great encouragement and have made this project complete.

To my kind and hardworking agent, Don Gates: Thank you for rooting for me and for this book! I'm grateful for your leadership, integrity, kindness, and counsel.

To the team at Bethany House: Thank you for your immediate zeal over the message of *Fight Your Fears* and your desire to give it a platform. It's been a joy serving our Lord Jesus alongside you.

To Andy McGuire: For your patient and helpful guidance and editing, *thank you*! Thanks also for being an advocate for this project from the very beginning and for believing that God's Word does God's work.

To Sharon Hodge: I am amazed by your skill and discernment—Bethany House is blessed to have you editing their projects. *Thank you* for catching my mistakes, encouraging me, and massively improving upon this work!

I often tell people about the gospel-centrality of our church and its commitment to Christ-exalting, Word-centered preaching and teaching. The Orchard Evangelical Free Church is imprinted all over these pages. Thank you, God, for our church!

My family has been praying for this project since its beginning. Thank you, Mom and Dad, for raising our family in the Word and for your constant support and love; and thank you, Katie Marie, for your care and prayers. Thanks to Dad W. for always asking about the process, and to Mom W. for your willingness to listen to chapter ideas. I love you all.

To my sweet girl, Joanna Grace: Being your mommy is my favorite job! You bring such sunshine to my days. One of our memory verses was on my mind a lot during this project: "She is clothed with strength and dignity, and she laughs without fear of the future" (Proverbs 31:25 NLT). I praise God for you, beautiful girl. Thanks for praying "blessings" over me these last six months!

To my husband, Brad: I am humbled by your love, kindness, and support. You spur me on to fear the Lord first and foremost, and also during long processes like writing this book. Thanks for encouraging me, and mostly for leading our family to fight the good fight of faith. I love you!

To my faithful Savior Jesus, who will never let me go: When I am afraid, I put my trust in you.

APPENDIX A

RECOMMENDED BOOKS

A GREAT WAY to grow in fighting fear is to read excellent books that are dripping with Scripture. Following is a list of my favorites. I commend them to you!

On the attributes of God:

- *Knowing God* by J. I. Packer
- *Evangelism and the Sovereignty of God* by J. I. Packer
- *The Holiness of God* by R. C. Sproul
- *The Sovereignty of God* by A. W. Pink
- *The Knowledge of the Holy* by A.W. Tozer
- *The Joy of Fearing God* by Jerry Bridges
- *Desiring God: Meditations of a Christian Hedonist* by John Piper
- *None Like Him: 10 Ways God Is Different from Us (and Why That's a Good Thing)* by Jen Wilkin

On the atonement and the gospel:

- *The Cross of Christ* by John Stott
- *Heaven, How I Got Here: The Story of the Thief on the Cross* by Colin S. Smith
- *From Good to Grace: Letting Go of the Goodness Gospel* by Christine Hoover
- *Gospel Deeps: Reveling in the Excellencies of Jesus* by Jared C. Wilson

On holiness:

- *The Practice of Godliness* by Jerry Bridges
- *The Pursuit of Holiness* by Jerry Bridges
- *Spiritual Depression: Its Causes and Cure* by Dr. Martyn Lloyd-Jones
- *When I Don't Desire God: How to Fight for Joy* by John Piper
- *In His Image: 10 Ways God Calls Us to Reflect His Character* by Jen Wilkin

On the Bible:

- *Reading the Bible Supernaturally: Seeing and Savoring the Glory of God in Scripture* by John Piper
- *10 Keys for Unlocking the Bible: Treasures That Will Change Your Life* by Colin S. Smith
- *Women of the Word: How to Study the Bible with Both Our Hearts and Our Minds* by Jen Wilkin

On fear:

- *Triumphing over Sinful Fear* by John Flavel
- *Trusting God: Even When Life Hurts* by Jerry Bridges
- *Running Scared: Fear, Worry, and the God of Rest* by Edward T. Welch
- *When People Are Big and God Is Small* by Edward T. Welch
- *Fear and Faith: Finding the Peace Your Heart Craves* by Trillia J. Newbell

APPENDIX B

SCRIPTURE MEMORY CARDS

C UT OUT THE CARDS on the following pages to help you memorize ten key verses from this book.

The *friendship*
of the Lord
is for those who *fear* him,
and he makes known
to them his COVENANT.

PSALM 25:14

FIGHT YOUR FEARS

There is therefore now
no condemnation
for those who are
in Christ Jesus.

ROMANS 8:1

FIGHT YOUR FEARS

My counsel
shall stand,
and *I* will accomplish
all my PURPOSE.

ISAIAH 46:10

FIGHT YOUR FEARS

The *young lions*
suffer want and hunger;
but those who seek the Lord
lack no *good thing.*

PSALM 34:10

FIGHT YOUR FEARS

Fear not,
little flock,
for it is your Father's
good pleasure
to give you the
kingdom.

LUKE 12:32

FIGHT YOUR FEARS

The Lord will keep you
from all evil;
he will keep your life.
The Lord will keep
your going out
and your coming in
from this time forth and
forevermore.

PSALM 121:7-8

FIGHT YOUR FEARS

God has said,
"Never
will I leave you;
never
will I forsake you."

HEBREWS 13:5

FIGHT YOUR FEARS

And to the one
who does not work
but believes *in him*
who justifies the ungodly,
his faith is counted as
righteousness.

ROMANS 4:5

FIGHT YOUR FEARS

For we must all *appear* before the judgment seat of Christ, so that each one may *receive* what is due for what he has done in the body, whether *good* or *evil*.

2 CORINTHIANS 5:10

FIGHT YOUR FEARS

Jesus said to her, "*I am* the *resurrection* and the *life*. Whoever believes in me, though he die, yet shall he live, and *everyone* who lives and believes in me shall never die. Do you *believe* this?"

JOHN 11:25-26

FIGHT YOUR FEARS

NOTES

Introduction: From One Fearful Person to Another

1. Colin S. Smith, *Women of Faith in a Culture of Fear* (Barrington, IL: Unlocking the Bible, 2016), 30–31.

Chapter 1: I Am God (When You Aren't Afraid Enough)

1. Jonathan Edwards, "A Divine and Supernatural Light," in *A Jonathan Edwards Reader*, ed. John E. Smith, Harry S. Stout, and Kenneth P. Minkema (New Haven, CT: Yale University Press, 1995), 119.

2. John Calvin, *Calvin: Institutes of the Christian Religion, Volume 1*, ed. John T. McNeill, trans. Ford Lewis Battles (Louisville, KY: Westminster John Knox Press, 2006), 39.

3. The best resource I've read on God's enjoyment of himself in the Trinity is John Piper's *Desiring God*.

4. Read Genesis 3 to feel the full weight of this tragedy.

5. John Flavel, *Triumphing over Sinful Fear* (Grand Rapids, MI: Reformation Heritage Books, 2011), 8.

6. Jon Bloom, "Lord, Set Me Free from Fear," *Desiring God*, February 12, 2018, https://www.desiringgod.org/articles/lord-set-me-free-from-fear.

7. Colin S. Smith, "Our First Impulse after We Sin," *Unlocking the Bible*, November 7, 2018, https://unlockingthebible.org/lifekey/our-first-impulse-after-we-sin.

8. John R.W. Stott, *The Cross of Christ*, 20th anniversary ed. (Downers Grove, IL: InterVarsity Press, 2006), 107.

9. R.C. Sproul, *The Holiness of God*, 2nd rev. and expanded ed. (Carol Stream, IL: Tyndale Momentum, 2000), 176.

Chapter 2: I Have Saved You (When You Fear Condemnation)

1. Matthew Henry, *Matthew Henry's Commentary on the Whole Bible: Complete and Unabridged in One Volume* (Peabody, MA: Hendrickson Publishers, 1994), 126, CD-ROM.

2. See Matthew 17, Mark 9, and Luke 9 for transfiguration accounts.

3. John R.W. Stott, *The Cross of Christ*, 20th anniversary ed. (Downers Grove, IL: InterVarsity Press, 2006), 109.

4. Stott, *The Cross of Christ*, 71.

5. Stott, *The Cross of Christ*, 71.

6. More on this in chapter 8.

7. Henry, *Commentary on the Whole Bible*, 1701.

Chapter 3: I Am Sovereign (When You Fear Not Being in Control)

1. I am indebted to my senior pastor, Colin Smith, for this insightful truth, which he often reminds our church of when he preaches. It's changed the way I read my Bible!

2. Jerry Bridges, *Trusting God: Even When Life Hurts* (Colorado Springs, CO: NavPress, 1988), 34.

3. A.W. Tozer, *The Knowledge of the Holy* (New York: HarperCollins Publishers, 1961), 108.

4. Bridges, *Trusting God*, 67.

5. One of the best teachings I've heard on this is from Colin Smith's sermon "How to Overcome Your Fears." This, along with his book *Women of Faith in a Culture of Fear*, has greatly informed my thoughts on why we're afraid of not being in control. Access the sermon at Unlocking the Bible's website: http://unlockingthebible.org.

6. John R.W. Stott, *The Cross of Christ*, 20th anniversary ed. (Downers Grove, IL: InterVarsity Press, 2006), 331.

7. Bridges, *Trusting God*, 104.

8. Tozer, *The Knowledge of the Holy*, 110.

9. For more reading on this topic, see John Piper's *Spectacular Sins: And Their Global Purpose in the Glory of Christ* and A. W. Pink's *The Sovereignty of God*.

Chapter 4: I Am Good (When You Fear the Worst)

1. Beth Wetherell, *Our Help: Four Young Children, Two with Cancer, One Magnificent Promise* (self-pub., CreateSpace, 2014), 33–34.

2. Talk to someone about this, preferably a biblical counselor, as anxiety that feels uncontrollable can be addressed. You might ask your pastor for a referral, or visit the Christian Counseling & Educational Foundation at https://www.ccef.org/ for resources.

3. *Merriam-Webster*, s.v. "Doubt," accessed December 2018, https://www.merriam-webster.com/dictionary/doubt.

4. J. I. Packer, *Knowing God* (Downers Grove, IL: InterVarsity Press, 1993), 161.

5. Sam Allberry, "You Need Not Worry About Next Year," *Desiring God*, December 28, 2018, https://www.desiringgod.org/articles/you-need-not-worry-about-next-year.

6. Packer, *Knowing God*, 270.

7. Packer, *Knowing God*, 165.

8. Wetherell, *Our Help*, 167–68.

Chapter 5: I Will Provide (When You Fear You Won't Have Enough)

1. Trent Hamm, "The Fear of Returning to Poverty," *The Simple Dollar*, updated August 17, 2017, accessed January 2019, https://www.thesimpledollar.com/the-fear-of-returning-to-poverty.

2. Jen Wilkin, *None Like Him: 10 Ways God Is Different from Us (and Why That's a Good Thing)* (Wheaton, IL: Crossway, 2016), 59.

3. See Matthew 26:6–13 and Luke 16:19–31 as two examples.

4. See Mark 8:34 and 10:30, 2 Corinthians 1:5, and 2 Timothy 2:3 as some examples.

5. Matthew Henry, "Commentary on Luke 12," Blue Letter Bible, accessed January 2019, https://www.blueletterbible.org/Comm/mhc/Luk/Luk_012.cfm?a=985031.

6. John Flavel, *Triumphing over Sinful Fear* (Grand Rapids, MI: Reformation Heritage Books, 2011), 84.

Chapter 6: I Will Protect You (When You Fear Evil)

1. Jerry Bridges, *Trusting God: Even When Life Hurts* (Colorado Springs, CO: NavPress, 1988), 65.

2. John Piper, "Satan's Ten Strategies Against You," *Desiring God*, October 4, 2016, https://www.desiringgod.org/articles/satans-ten-strategies-against-you.

3. J. I. Packer, *Knowing God* (Downers Grove, IL: InterVarsity Press, 1993), 151.

Chapter 7: I Will Never Leave You (When You Fear Loneliness)

1. John T. Cacioppo and William Patrick, *Loneliness: Human Nature and the Need for Social Connection* (New York: W.W. Norton & Company, 2008), 5.

2. Ben Sasse, *Them: Why We Hate Each Other—and How to Heal* (New York: St. Martin's Press, 2018), 23.

3. Sasse, *Them*, 29.

4. Lydia Brownback, *Finding God in My Loneliness* (Wheaton, IL: Crossway, 2017), 15.

5. Brownback, *Finding God*, 14.

6. Caitlin Plascencia (Hope When It Hurts), "Caitlin's Story of Hope When It Hurts," Facebook, January 24, 2017, https://www.facebook.com/hopewhenit hurts/photos/a.1856796207891228/1875253686045480/?type=3&theater.

7. Plascencia, "Caitlin's Story."

8. Katie Evensen, email message to author, January 30, 2019. Used with permission.

9. Evensen, email.

10. Email message to author, April 25, 2019. Used with permission.

11. Email message to author.

12. Email message to author.

13. Felicity Carswell, email message to author, February 4, 2019. Used with permission.

14. Carswell, email.

15. Carswell, email.

16. Kristen Wetherell and Sarah Walton, *Hope When It Hurts: Biblical Reflections to Help You Grasp God's Purpose in Your Suffering* (Surrey, UK: The Good Book Company, 2017), 109–10.

17. Wetherell and Walton, *Hope When It Hurts*, 111–12.

18. Flavel, *Triumphing over Sinful Fear*, 64–65.

Chapter 8: I Have Accepted You (When You Fear Failure)

1. Colin S. Smith, "Curse," January 13, 2019, in *Open: A One-Year Journey through the Bible*, the Orchard Evangelical Free Church, video, https://the

orchardefc.org/home/sermons-resources/sermons/view-sermon/?sermon_i
d=31934.

2. John Calvin, *Calvin: Institutes of the Christian Religion, Volume 1*, ed.
John T. McNeill, trans. Ford Lewis Battles (Louisville, KY: Westminster John
Knox Press, 2006), 726.

3. Romans is my favorite book of the Bible. I highly encourage you to read it
with Paul's background in mind. You'll be gripped, as he was, by the gospel that
is "the power of God for salvation to everyone who believes" (Romans 1:16).

4. Jared C. Wilson, *The Imperfect Disciple: Grace for People Who Can't Get
Their Act Together* (Grand Rapids, MI: Baker Books, 2017), 50.

Chapter 9: I Will Judge You (When You Fear Man)

1. Edward T. Welch, *When People Are Big and God Is Small: Overcoming
Peer Pressure, Codependency, and the Fear of Man* (Philipsburg, NJ: P&R Publishing, 1997), 14.

2. J. I. Packer, *Knowing God* (Downers Grove, IL: InterVarsity Press, 1993),
141.

3. Packer, *Knowing God*, 141.

4. R.C. Sproul, *The Holiness of God*, 2nd rev. expanded ed. (Carol Stream,
IL: Tyndale Momentum, 2000), 108.

Chapter 10: I Am Alive (When You Fear Death)

1. Colin S. Smith, "Immediacy: What Will It Be Like in Heaven?" April 19,
2015, in *Heaven*, video, Unlocking the Bible, https://unlockingthebible.org
/sermon/immediacy-what-will-it-be-like-in-heaven.

2. Charles Spurgeon, "Dying Daily," the Spurgeon Center, August 29, 1868,
accessed April 2019, https://www.spurgeon.org/resource-library/sermons
/dying-daily.

3. John Calvin, *Calvin: Institutes of the Christian Religion, Volume 1*, ed.
John T. McNeill, trans. Ford Lewis Battles (Louisville, KY: Westminster John
Knox Press, 2006), 198–99.

4. James Merritt, "No Fear," October 10, 2000, the Gospel Coalition, podcast
audio, https://resources.thegospelcoalition.org/library/no-fear.

5. "Lord's Day 1," Heidelberg Catechism, accessed April 2019, http://www
.heidelberg-catechism.com/en/lords-days/1.html.

6. Colin S. Smith, "Six Dimensions of Hell on the Cross," Unlocking the
Bible, April 22, 2015, https://unlockingthebible.org/2015/04/six-dimensions
-of-hell-on-the-cross.

7. Colin S. Smith, *Heaven, How I Got Here: The Story of the Thief on the Cross* (Scotland, UK: Christian Focus Publications, 2015), 83.

8. See also Philippians 1:21–23 and Luke 23:43.

9. Edward T. Welch, *Running Scared: Fear, Worry, and the God of Rest* (Greensboro, NC: New Growth Press, 2007), 236–38.

10. I get this word *outrage* from Don Carson's insight on these verses in his sermon "Lazarus," given on April 3, 2019 at the Gospel Coalition's 2019 National Conference: https://www.thegospelcoalition.org/conference_media /lazarus/.

11. William R. Moody, *The Life of Dwight L. Moody* (Chicago, IL: Fleming H. Revell Company, 1900), v.

KRISTEN WETHERELL is a wife, mother, and writer. She is the coauthor of the award-winning book *Hope When It Hurts: Biblical Reflections to Help You Grasp God's Purpose in Your Suffering.* Kristen lives in Chicagoland with her husband, Brad, and their daughter.

YOUR NOTES